FIVE
PRINCIPLES
FOR A MEANINGFUL, FRUITFUL LIFE

Christopher Clay

Published by Argyle Fox Publishing | argylefoxpublishing.com

Publisher holds no responsibility for content of this work.
Content is the sole responsibility of the author.

ISBN 978-1-953259-55-4 (Paperback)
ISBN 978-1-953259-80-6 (Hardcover)
ISBN 978-1-953259-81-3 (Ebook)

I dedicate this book to

Jonathon, Justin, Elizabeth, and Evelyn—
live deep and meaningful lives.
To my parents, whose guidance brought this book to life.
To my wife, who always pushes me to be better.
And to friends and family who supported this book.

TABLE OF CONTENTS

FIVE
PRINCIPLES

ARGYLE FOX
PUBLISHING

ACKNOWLEDGMENTS

I would like to thank Jesus, the Messiah, for his constant mercy and redeeming grace; my wife, Stephanie, for being my true companion; Paul and Linda Clay, my parents, for their invaluable guidance; my children (and wife) for giving me the space and time to write; and Kristi Atha-Rader for being a great business partner and leader who helped develop these ideas in a corporate setting and influenced these principles from an organizational perspective. This book was originally going to be a business book outlining how we built a successful, thriving health care company in West Virginia. It became something a little different. Additionally, I am thankful for Rainelle Medical Center, the board, and staff for the opportunity to work with them, grow, and develop within the company—particularly Lisa Dennison, Cindy Harris, Robert Saul, and Sarah Nolen. I am grateful to Daniel Brantley with Argyle Fox Publishing for his support, editing, and publishing wisdom; my dear friends Maga Kisriev and Jason Ratliff for their feedback and insight; Jonathan Wright, Gina Mushynsky, and Cindy Harris for their editing help. Thank you, dear reader—your actions to live a more meaningful and fruitful life make the world a better place.

INTRODUCTION TO PRINCIPLES

Now of first principles we see some by induction, some by perception, some by a certain habituation, and others too in other ways. But each set of principles we must try to investigate in the natural way, and we must take pains to state them definitely, since they have a great influence on what follows. For the beginning is thought to be more than half of the whole, and many of the questions we ask are cleared up by it.

—Aristotle, Nicomachean Ethics, Book I

There are three constants in life: change, choice, and principles.

—Stephen Covey

Five Principles is about building a meaningful life by developing character. It rejects the world's values of appearance, charisma, bliss, and noise that lead to empty failure. If you want a meaningful life, healthy relationships, and genuine success, these principles are for you. Principles are the foundation on which you build character, and applying *Five Principles* to your life will make you healthier, smarter, more balanced, and enlightened.

Principles are the foundation for a belief system. You have principles you live by, consciously and unconsciously, because you believe things. You believe the sun will rise in the morning, food provides energy, your spouse loves you, and a thousand other things throughout the day. These beliefs are principles or algorithms that help with decision-making.

The belief that you need eight hours of sleep allows you to calculate the proper time to go to sleep. You believe your spouse loves you, therefore you confide in them. You believe the grocer would not sell you poisoned food, so you eat food from the grocer without questioning the contents.

Religion, math, economics, business, science, health, and combat—they all offer principles to live by. Some principles are laws unto themselves. Break them (if you can) and expect great consequences. Other principles can be cute, naive, or poorly thought out, ultimately serving as foundations for destruction and pain. Some can serve as a foundation for meaningful success and happiness. Those are the principles discussed in this book.

You are an individual with individual purposes, skills, relationships, environments, and resources. As an individual, you choose your core principles. Whether you choose them intentionally or have them imposed upon you, you are still choosing.

Here are five good principles to choose:
• Purpose: Live purposefully.
• Skills: Work to develop skill.
• People: Value people and build relationships.
• Environment: Position where value can be added.
• Resources: Use resources with discipline.

These principles can be used individually, in relationships, and in broader communities (religious, business, educational, governmental, etc.). Together, they make an interwoven fabric for success. Miss one and the others weaken.

A business that provides a high-quality product (purpose) but ignores what the market (people) wants will fail. Contrast that against a business with a clear purpose and skill to execute on that purpose, leadership that understands and serves the market (people), is positioned to differentiate the company within its industry (environment), and effective resource allocation. That business will succeed.

The more interwoven the principles, the more powerful they become. With effort and time, you can weave them together to discover a more meaningful and successful life.

In the diagrams that follow, success is indicated by a tree. It's most fruitful in the intersection of purpose, skill, people, environment, and resources.

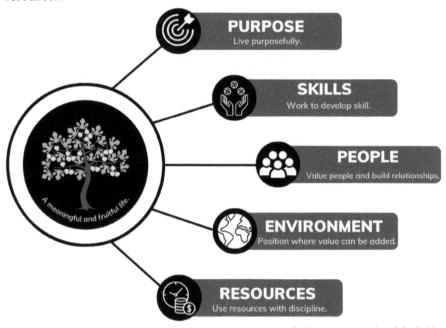

If you apply these principles—live purposefully, use and build skills toward that purpose, understand your weaknesses while serving people, navigate and lead within your environment, and leverage the resources of your time, money, and knowledge—you will find success.

These principles are found in other writings. However, we all struggle and need grace. When we aim to live in harmonious, loving, conscious, and disciplined ways, we seek the higher path. This path toward a meaningful life requires action.

The best myths and stories create a resonate story by mapping principles onto the actions or words of characters. Humankind cannot hear God speak without mapping his words to life. Communication with the divine always creates religion. Real spirituality flows from foundationally strong religion. All good principles lead to truth based in the Word.

Humankind knows so little, and there is much to learn. The challenge is to codify goals, laws, and principles into your personal and individual life. After all, it's one thing to know principles, but it's another altogether to live by them.

Do you become a monk, seek a Wall Street-tycoon lifestyle, live for the moment, or plan out your day? Using principles to build a meaningful life will uncover answers to those questions.

In essence, your principles help you focus in a noisy world.

PART I
PURPOSE

Chapter 1

MEANING

He who has a why *to live for can bear almost any* how.

—Friedrich Nietzsche

The mystery of human existence lies not in just staying alive, but in finding something to live for.

—Fyodor Dostoyevsky, *The Brothers Karamazov*

Meaning

Purpose involves knowing your own skills, people, environment, and personal resources. Yet, purpose transcends all of these. It comes first and last. It is the beginning and the end.

Modern culture has much to say about passion. "Find your passion and you will never work a day of your life!" "Follow your passion!" Exciting as such encouragement may be, it is terrible advice. Passion is an emotional reaction. You could passionately love a song, but listen to it at top volume day and night for a week and you might go mad. You need a better path!

Purpose transcends passion. This chapter focuses on purpose in its broader sense of meaning or truth. For a life lived by principles, you must first focus on meaning or truth.

"What does it profit a man to gain the whole world, yet forfeit his soul? For what could a man give in exchange for his soul?" (Mark 8:36–37 TLV)

If this life is all there is, why care about purpose, meaning, legacy, or anything else? It's all meaningless. However, few people confronted with absolute meaninglessness remain sane. Head down that path and you'll reach a dark place. You must come to an understanding of meaning, because a meaningless life is a lost life. If this is where you are, you must confront it.

Stories

How do you confront meaninglessness? The sages have asked this question for ages, and their answers are found in some of our greatest philosophical texts, stories, and writings.

At a basic level, humans crave meaning. It is unsurprising when a person struggling with meaninglessness is sad and discontented. Human nature demands meaning. The story of humanity is one of seeking meaning. You are a meaning-creating being!

In *Sapiens*, Yuval Noah Harari argues that what made Homo sapiens (modern humans) able to rise above their counterparts (Homo neanderthalensis and Homo erectus) is the ability to tell and find meaning in stories. The stories we tell ourselves of gods, nations, economies, and ideas allow us to rise above mere animals and cooperate in powerful ways.

Meaning drives human action. At a basic and evolutionary level, your meaning is to survive, propagate, and pass on your genetic code. Yet you desire more than this. You ask *why*? Why survive, propagate, and pass on genetic code? For approximately a million years, our archaic ancestors Homo erectus existed. Eventually, erectus gave rise to the species sapiens. Yet for much of this time, our species was not special.

We existed alongside other species of the genus Homo and animals. While we did, we merely survived. Then something happened fifty thousand years ago. We started telling stories and believing them; we acknowledged chaos and determined to make order. Ancient hieroglyphs and cave drawings provide proof of these early stores. From the first tales told, stories enable us to reshape and master the world—to not merely survive, but give life meaning. You are on a purposeful mission millions of years in the making.

You desire meaning or you would not get up, go to work, bother with relationships, or raise a family. In the first book and chapter of the Bible, you find the commandment to "Be fruitful and multiply" (Genesis 1:28 NKJV). This is a basic biological imperative: continue to exist. Your biology contains meaning. It's a simple fact you can see and understand.

Yet meaning is more than biology, and it is more than procreation. As the only storytelling and story-believing species, our stories are the key to meaning. You can tell yourself a story about what it means to "Be fruitful and multiply." The beauty and terror is that the stories you choose to tell and believe matter!

How can you know what stories to tell and believe? Why, with a story you tell yourself. Here is the first part of that story. Tell yourself that the stories you believe and tell matter. If you cannot tell yourself a story and believe it and if you cannot believe stories you are told, you are—to borrow from *Forrest Gump*—a feather on the wind.

Speaking of *Forrest Gump*—if you believe the *Forrest Gump* story, you have not read, heard, and studied enough stories. Such false stories lead down dangerous paths. Allow me to give you a few stories that need careful consideration—"The Epic of Gilgamesh," the stories told by Socrates and Plato, and all Holy Scripture. These are good places to start.

The ancient Mesopotamian poem "The Epic of Gilgamesh" recounts the adventures of the king of Uruk and his friend Enkidu. These stories teach that attaining wisdom and kindness is more important than gaining immortality. They also teach that death is inevitable. Wisdom and kindness can only be more important than your biological imperative to survive and procreate if you believe what "The Epic of Gilgamesh" is teaching. If you believe the story that wisdom and kindness are more important than your biological imperative, you can believe in stories.

Socrates, one of the fathers of philosophy, teaches that we are all ignorant, himself included, and the oracle professes him to be the wisest man of all. In his famous "Allegory of the Cave," Plato claims you must break free from the chains of ignorance and embark on a journey into the unknown. You must stop being deceived by your senses and ignorance. You must learn, grow, and behold that which is meaningful and of a higher reality. If you can believe that, then you can tell yourself stories of breaking free from the chains of ignorance, stories that insist wisdom and kindness are obtainable, and stories that it's possible to seek a higher reality. Framed this way, "Allegory of the Cave" is not simply a story about breaking free, but striving for the upmost limits of wisdom and kindness. What level of higher reality can you believe and share?

At the deepest level, the Holy Scriptures tell of a higher reality—God, paradise, heaven, and enlightenment. These are stories of a Being, place, and reality at the limits of, and beyond, your ability to comprehend. However, these stories beg us to strive and reach for the unknowable: salvation, enlightenment, and paradise. These stories transcend biology, science, and the material world. They explain that what you do matters beyond here and now. These stories speak to meaning beyond yourself, time, and the world.

If you believe stories matter, what stories should you believe and tell? The consequences are steep because the devil and fools are storytellers.

No one can tell another person all the stories they need to believe and tell. However, you know a meaningful story when you hear it. Paul tells the Romans to "glory in tribulations, knowing that tribulations produce perseverance; and perseverance, character; and character, hope" (Romans 5:3 NKJV). The famous Roman philosopher Seneca wrote to a friend, "I judge you unfortunate because you have never lived through misfortune. You have passed through life without an opponent—no one can ever know what you are capable of, not even you."

What does a wonderful story embody? An arc. Humanity needs suffering. You need something to strive for and struggle against. You need a goal toward which to aim.

If procreation is a biological imperative, then protection must follow for a species with limited ability to produce offspring. Again, our biology calls us to a story—a story of confronting the difficult. Protection is fighting, striving, working, and suffering to create a world tomorrow better than the world today.

Maybe you have a good life right now. You have money to purchase this book and free time and energy to read. Life is stable, perhaps headed in the right direction. The comfortable person may answer, "Who cares about meaning? Not me. Eat, drink, and be merry!" But what happens when the drink runs out, there's no food on the table, those you care about betray you, or you get ill, and the suffering begins?

Meaninglessness and suffering combined lead to chaos and destruction. A look at school shootings during the beginning of the twenty-first century reveals the consequences of a society raised in a vacuum of morality or meaninglessness in a world filled with suffering. The conclusion of such a story contains no beauty. If you find yourself in this place, seek help.

Modern culture reduces everything to science, the *how* of the world. Unfortunately, science cannot deal with the most important question: *Why?* Modernity says the material is of primary concern, but this is a lie. Materialists misunderstand reality. The most important things are intangible: friendship, love, beauty, self, and the Divine. Humanity's story is most beautiful where it transcends science, rises above biology, and believes in a higher reality. Don't get me wrong. The natural world is important. Yet other things are more important.

You find meaning in struggle, in the difficult and hard, in denying yourself to seek truth. You suffer in childbirth, when learning sports, in study, or navigating social dynamics in school or work. Growth typically requires pain, figuratively and literally. Stop growing, and you'll either die or fall behind.

You do not overcome true difficulty with ease, and you can avoid suffering only temporarily. Therefore, your only option is, in military parlance, to "embrace the suck." Be brave. Have faith. Turn toward suffering. Take up your cross. Assent to truth.

Pain, fear, suffering, and chaos reside in the unknown. Why do people fear the dark? Because what is there is unknown. Confront it, and you can deal with it. You can learn and grow. Maybe there is a monster, but maybe it is a mouse. Until you confront it and embrace it, you will never know.

Finding meaning by confronting suffering is a powerful story to tell yourself. Your story will give you meaning if it pushes you to do something hard and consequently grow. If something is hard to learn, causes you to be criticized and feel emotional discomfort, tests your physical and mental limits, and challenges your will and spirit, it will be meaningful.

President John F. Kennedy understood this, and it motivated a nation to reach for one of the most meaningful achievements in all human history—landing on the moon.

> But why, some say, the Moon? Why choose this as our goal? And they may well ask, why climb the highest mountain? Why, 35 years ago, fly the Atlantic? Why does Rice play Texas? *We choose to go to the Moon.* We choose to go to the Moon . . . We choose to go to the Moon in this decade and do the other things, not because they are easy, but because they are hard; because that goal will serve to organize and measure the best of our energies and skills, because that challenge is one that we are willing to accept.

You can confront suffering at multiple levels. First, you must answer it at an individual level. You "glory in tribulation," do what is hard, and get after it. Second, you answer it in relationships by loving, forgiving, and accepting others. Third, you do it in community and society by being an example—shining a light in the darkness and telling your story.

The individual level is most important because it enables you to confront suffering elsewhere. However, the individual level is complex. You are a physical, mental, emotional, and spiritual being with unique traits and dichotomies as varied as they are similar. Therefore, you must start with yourself if you are to affect those around you and eventually expand your "circles of influence" (Covey, 1985). You must confront suffering in your life before worrying about others and society.

Scary, I know. However, pain and suffering are a part of life. By choosing your *why*, your *meaning*, your *hard*, you learn to face the suffering. Then you can manage, reduce, and/or cope with it. Doing this takes away its power, ultimately reducing suffering. You make the world a better place when your life purpose is to do that which is meaningful. What is the most meaningful thing you can do in your life?

Summary

Life is hard. The longer you deny this and seek the broad path, the less meaning you will find. Unfortunately, many refuse to accept this reality and constantly expect it to get easier or better. They are victims, feathers on the wind. They're buffeted by fate, taken advantage of, abused, and confused by a world they will never understand.

This book is about a different path. Life is about serving a purpose, which means taking responsibility for yourself and facing the difficult things in life. When you do, you may overcome them. At the least, you will learn to live with them.

Each part of this book (Purpose, Skill, People, Environment, and Resources) addresses how you can best use the associated principles in your life individually, the lives of those close to you, and in the broader communities you seek to serve—particularly business but also society, government, and other organizations. This order is important. If you cannot face the difficult things in your own life, how can you expect to help your spouse, child, or business associate with their suffering? If

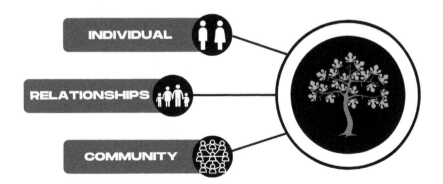

your own relationships are not in order, how can you serve your church, employees, business, city, or country in any meaningful way?

Living a life of purpose and skill that is people-focused, value-based, and resource-conscious requires action. And meaningful action is hard. It is hard to live meaningfully on a consistent basis. I know this firsthand. Because while I try to live by these principles daily, I fail repeatedly.

Think of this like training for a marathon. You cannot run a marathon without training. You first learn to jog a mile, then two, and then three. Then you begin running. When you can run a few miles, you jog even farther. You give your body time to rest. As you work on increasing your distance, you also increase your speed. You add in strength training as well. Through the months of training, every mile won't be faster and every run won't be longer. There will be breaks, staggered distances, slower and faster paces, strength training, flexibility training, and rest. But you keep at it, focused on your goal and plan.

Living a principled life of meaning is much the same. You cannot start from another's path or an arbitrary starting location. This makes sense in running. If you cannot run six miles, 26.2 miles—a full marathon—is out of the question. Apply this same principle to life. You may desire success right now, but you must train first.

What do you do when you fall down? I ask my kids this often. Now, I ask you the same. Suffering will knock you down. Live by the principles in this book and there will be pain, suffering, and falling. Don't give up. Get up.

Chapter 2

SELF

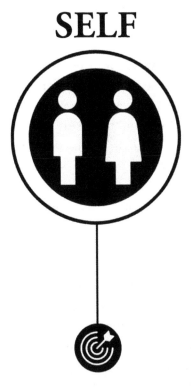

There is nothing noble in being superior to your fellow men. True nobility lies in being superior to your former self.

—Ernest Hemingway

The highest manifestation of life consists in this: that a being governs its own actions. A thing which is always subject to the direction of another is somewhat of a dead thing.

—Thomas Aquinas

Begin with Self

You probably cannot cure cancer tomorrow. If you can, please do. Typically, you'll start smaller, with yourself. Confront the suffering in your individual life, particularly the suffering you cause.

Humans are bodies, minds, hearts, and spirit. This is the paradigm or pattern of being—the physical, the body; the mental, the mind; the emotional, the heart (or soul); and the spiritual, the existential, eternal self.

Your physical body involves your health status, the shelter in which you live, and the resources available to you for food, shelter, and clothing. Your mind is your mental capacity and sanity. The mind desires growth, health, and purpose. Boredom and crisis are two extremes that cause serious suffering of the mind if not confronted with seriousness and urgency. Your heart is your emotional status guided by relationships with yourself and others. Emotional distress has many causes, ranging from chemical imbalances to misunderstandings about your place in the world. Likewise, poor relationships can affect you and cause suffering outside yourself. Finally, spirit is most important and can be hardest to address. It is hard to worry about the bigger "spiritual" picture while the body, mind, or heart suffer. Conversely, addressing issues of the spirit can lend resilience to the body, heart, and mind. If you take on the purpose of decreasing suffering in the world, you can bear starvation without killing your fellow man, solitary confinement without going crazy, and great betrayal without causing bloody mayhem. Spirit, then, is something special beyond who and what you are in a physical, mental, and emotional sense.

Body

Your body is an engine that supplies your mind with oxygen and powers the actions of accomplishment. To confront suffering, you must first confront your own physical suffering. If you cannot, don't expect to master mental, emotional, and spiritual anguish. Face your physical limitations and suffering, seeking the hard things that will make you better.

Step 1

Garbage in, garbage out.

A diet helps you see food as fuel. The good ones change the way you think about food for the better. As Steve Kamb writes in his classic and constantly updated article, "What's the Best Diet to Lose Weight?", calorie-counting, low-carb, keto, paleo, intermittent fasting, and countless other diets are useful.

Ultimately, there are three rules for healthy eating: (1) eat mostly fresh, proper food, (2) eat only the amount needed for fuel, and (3) do this for your whole life. Any healthy diet reduces calories so the body learns to function on the proper amount of calories necessary for fuel. The diet that teaches you to think of food as fuel will win.

It's best to think of a diet as the way you eat. If you go with the keto diet, don't tell yourself that you're on a diet. Tell yourself that you avoid eating carbs. It is a simple algorithm—no sugar, no bread, no starch, few carbs. This reduces calories and controls quality with a simple change in thinking. With the paleo diet, tell yourself that you eat fresh, unprocessed foods. Just watching calories? Your story is that you keep your calories under a set threshold. Again, good eating methods should be simple (Kamb 11).

Another powerful way to discipline the body is fasting. In the modern West we have an overabundance of foods. Many of these foods are full of poor content and cheap calories. Now, we are seeing the consequences of the export of cheap calories and sugar, as otherwise healthy indigenous people contract chronic health problems previously unexperienced in their societies. Fasting offers a forced break from food addictions you may not know you have.

Over the past decade, more research has shown the benefits of fasting. It helps with neurodegenerative diseases like Alzheimer's and Parkinson's by "activating adaptive stress responses" that protect neurons from accumulating amyloid plaques (Sugarman 2016). Fasting also reduces insulin resistance, fights inflammation, enhances heart health, improves brain function and mood, boosts metabolism, increases growth hormone secretion, and more (Link 2018).

For ages, spiritual disciplines have promoted fasting as beneficial. In the Quran, Ayah 183, are found these words: "O ye who believe! They prescribe fasting for you, even as it was prescribed for those before you, that ye may ward off evil." As the fourth Pillar of Islam (Aqidah), fasting provides spiritual, mental, and emotional benefits: "that ye may ward off evil."

Orthodox Christians hold fasts on 150 days of the year. Sin begins in the body, and sinful thinking leads to sinful action. Fasting teaches patience and self-control to the religious disciple. Desire and passion can easily run free in your heart and mind; a hungry belly focuses on patience and self-control. These are mental, emotional, and spiritual disciplines. Because fasts are often followed by feasts, fasting remind us of God's love for us.

Step 2

Muscle is better than fat.

Aerobic exercise powers the body, regulates cholesterol, and improves blood pressure. Strength (anaerobic) training slows aging, builds connective tissues, increases bone density, reduces the risk of injury, and eases arthritic pain. Together, aerobic and anaerobic exercise promote good health. Done an hour a day, exercise prepares you to confront suffering.

Why an hour? Thirty minutes helps maintain your fitness, but muscles store chemicals needed for energy (creatine phosphate and adenosine triphosphate). If you want to improve, deplete your energy stores. Depleting energy storage improves results by causing your muscles to burn excess proteins, carbohydrates, and fats and produce glucose to resupply the needed chemicals. Increased loads on your system signals the body to get stronger. Depending on the type of workout, it can take thirty minutes to deplete your storage. Some high-intensity workouts do this in twenty minutes, while low-intensity workouts take ninety minutes or longer. Therefore, the rule of thumb is to aim at a challenging, hour-long workout—especially for beginners.

If you want to do something meaningful, invest the time and effort. A workout planned for twenty minutes and knocked out in only ten provides minimum benefit. Sure, it's better than nothing, but not by much.

Train hard to stress your body. Sweat, experience discomfort, and push yourself every day. How hard should you push? Don't exercise so hard that you cannot exercise again for two or three days. That is self-defeating. Instead, aim for one percent improvement. These minor improvements equal enormous improvements through time.

While exercising, suffer for the sake of suffering. Consider it training for real suffering. Suffering through exercise opens the door to do something about the suffering in the world. If you can discipline the body to go beyond comfort into chaos, into the unknown (even just one percent further than before), into suffering, you can discipline the mind, heart, and spirit to do the same.

And don't neglect rest days. Just don't overdo it. Discipline expert Jocko Willink says, "Not today. With rest days, one should procrastinate." Avoid rest days when possible, knowing that suffering comes when you do not want it. Exercise should, therefore, come when you do not want it: early in the morning, after a hard day at the office, on vacation, during times of stress, on weekends, and during times of tragedy.

Finally, exercise every day, because a day off is poison, a lie, a sweet siren song. One day off turns into two, then a week, a month, and the rest of your life. You can see big lies coming. The small lie is most insidious. This does not mean that some competitive hoops with friends cannot be a substitute or that a good martial arts class cannot be fun. Exercise can be and should be fun, but you should show up for scheduled exercises whether or not you feel like it. You owe that to yourself, your training partners, or the team.

Step 3

Urgently and seriously address medical issues. If you do not have a doctor, get one. If you cannot afford a doctor, find a free clinic or health center that offers discounted fees.

The young and healthy need a baseline of health measurements, including blood pressure, resting heart rate, and basic labs. It is better to learn about potential health issues sooner rather than later! A good baseline allows you to spot issues in the future and address them in more meaningful ways.

Additionally, don't neglect having a primary care physician. A walk-in clinic can help when you can't access your doctor, but having a primary care physician makes your life better and longer. "Every 10 additional primary care physicians per 100,000 population was associated with a 51.5-day increase in life expectancy" (Basu 2019).

By knowing your health status, you're empowered to confront the suffering in your life today. The option is letting a problem fester until you die early, causing others to suffer. The monster in the closet is usually bigger than the monster in the light.

Mind

If you can develop your body, you can develop your mind. A sound mind is one of the most valuable assets you can have. While age weakens the body, your mind is more resilient, particularly as it regards crystallized intelligence. Evidence is mounting that you can slow aging, live longer, and maintain fluid intelligence into later life! Early evidence shows that mind exercises reduce the effects of Alzheimer's disease and dementia. With such potential, your mind deserves as much focus as your body. So, exercise it at least an hour every day.

There are many ways to exercise the mind. Experiment with mental exercises that fit your unique brain and best address your strengths and weaknesses. Whatever exercises you choose, they should include the following components:

- Meditation or prayer
- Listening, reading, or studying
- Creating or writing

Meditation allows you to both free and focus your mind. It takes a free and focused mind to break out of stuck thinking. Meditation comes in many forms—breathing exercises, transcendental relaxation, mindfulness, and prayer. We often think of prayer as talking to the divine, but it also includes listening to the divine.

When we listen to nature, natural law, the divine, and others, what might we learn? We will learn something that is going to challenge us and cause us to grow.

It is easier to renew and refocus a mindful mind free from attachment. Bruce Lee famously said, "Empty your cup so that it may be filled." A meditative or prayerful mind is open to new and challenging ideas.

How do you pray? All forms of meditation or prayer exercise discipline and take practice. The beautiful thing is that they do not take long to learn and, with a little practice, they become easier and more important to daily living. You just need quietness and detachment.

You are surrounded by the noise of entertainment in unlimited forms (music, movies, television, news, magazines, websites, podcasts, books, and social media) and nearly instant transportation. Technology carries this noise in your pocket, ear, wrist, and soon, embedded in your body. When learning to meditate, this noise is hard to overcome. Over time you learn to quiet the noise of the world and foster a prayerful mind amid chaos. However, at first you should practice in a quiet space. Carve out five to ten minutes each day to be intentionally quiet.

Quietness refers to the quietness of your mind. In fact, your mind provides more distraction than the noise of the world. You have so much information and noise floating around in your subconscious that it can be hard to be still and quiet. Do not become frustrated. Accept the distractions without emotion. Scratch the itch, pay the bill, contemplate the meeting, and move on. Let go of your attachment to whatever issue comes up.

This is the power of prayer. Prayer moves the focus from yourself and toward God. Over time, fewer and fewer subconscious distractions will arise. The more you discipline yourself to aligning your conscious and subconscious self, the healthier you become mentally. Keep your practice simple, focused, disciplined, and intentional.

Reading and studying are the next step in mental growth. When meditation and prayer precede a study session, your studying is more fruitful. Release preconceived ideas so you can learn new things.

Diligent and habitual study are necessary for mind development. Western culture is enamored with the idea that school is where you learn everything you need to know. The original point of education was to cultivate lifelong learners. Do not buy into the lie that you can stop learning. Failure to acknowledge your need to learn leads to pain and suffering!

What to study? This is a difficult question. Consider your individual strengths and weaknesses. Then use these as a starting place for your answer.

In business there is a term called "SWOT" analysis. It stands for strengths, weaknesses, opportunities, and threats. Strengths and weaknesses are internal, while opportunities and threats are external. A basketball player may be weak at defense but be a good shooter. This is a weakness and a strength (internal). His opponent may be taller but slow—both a threat and an opportunity (external). These categories can uncover areas to grow the mind Do you have strength to develop or weakness to mitigate?

When considering traits that are strengths or weaknesses, consider child-rearing. There are two common goals for raising children*— freedom to experiment and enforced character. If a child can develop passions and skills freely (freedom to experiment) yet have their character enforced (through parental and societal discipline) to develop those passions and skills honorably, the child is headed for success. When nearing adulthood, children should know their interests and passions. Typically, interests and passions are the things for which one has skills. These skills are strengths. As a child, you should have developed your strengths through experimental freedom and enforced character.

Adults who do not know their skills face a problem. There are several options to overcome this problem.

The first is to understand yourself psychologically. Are you driven, charismatic, compassionate, or analytical? There are various personality and social tests to help answer this question. Myers-Briggs, Five-Factor Model, DiSC, and others are excellent. Take time to learn about yourself; self-knowledge is a wonderful investment.

Next, look at what you are doing. If you have a job, there is obviously a need for this service, and you can perform this service. So, when you have a job, you have a strength. Despite what some say, no job done well is insignificant.

Take a humdrum job (whatever it is) and become world class at it.

Of course, there are more than two goals for raising children. But for our purposes, these two goals will suffice.

Check out library books, watch videos on best practices, research the best tools and supplies to use, and grow your mind for exactly what you are doing today! Within six months you will be the best employee holding that job the organization has ever employed. Within a year you will be the best in your region. Do that for ten years and you may be one of the best in the world.

This can happen with any occupation. Products, technologies, and knowledge within janitorial services are massive and expanding. A Google search recently pulled up 104,000 janitorial service videos. Amazon lists over 10,000 results for books on cleaning. A Bing search list has over 37,500,000 websites for cleaning products. These lists grow each month.

Mental growth starts with your strengths—pushing and developing them. As you master strengths, knowledge about weaknesses is helpful. Embarking into unknown territory can be a fearful thing. But the payoff can be immense.

To get started, admit your specific weaknesses. Personality profiles can be helpful here. If you lack empathy but have a driven personality, work on empathy. If you are a caring person but struggle with motivation or discipline, you know what needs improvement. Working on weaknesses is hard and unpleasant work. Ignore them, and they'll become dangerous blind spots.

Mental development also requires knowledge of opportunities and threats. What opportunities exist in your individual spiritual, physical, and emotional world? What environmental threats exist to your physical, emotional, and spiritual self? Answering these questions often takes imagination. Stories can create powerful connections. This is why we watch sports and why our favorite movies typically play out a healthy balance of opportunity and threat.

To find stories that help you process opportunities and threats, start with older stories first. The Lindy effect, which proposes that the life expectancy of a non-perishable variable is a function of the variables' current age, suggests such an approach. I learned about this in Nassim Taleb's book *Antifragile*:

So I follow the Lindy effect as a guide in selecting what to read: books that have been around for ten years will be around for ten more; books that have been around for two millennia should be around for quite a bit of time, and so forth.

The ultimate puzzle piece for developing the mind may seem like the oddest. Yet it can be the most powerful. You create to learn, even in the simplest of forms, written language; you take what is metaphysical—an idea or mental construct—and write it down physically. The words you're reading were once confined to my mind. They now exist here, printed on paper. This process teaches that creation is a learning process, because no individual or situation is the same. Whether building a supercomputer, writing the greatest novel of all time, or learning to write, you are creating and learning as you go.

The proper pursuit of knowledge challenges you, but not all study is suffering. Just as a runner becomes accustomed to a certain pace or distance, the mind does the same. You cannot leap from reading your first book to a complete understanding of Chaucer or Kant. As runners cannot run marathons every day, your mind cannot operate at full learning capacity for hours on end. The best runners implement easier runs and harder runs to stay in shape and prepare for the marathon. Consistency is what's important. Just like the marathoner on a relaxing six-mile jog, learners should recuperate with entertaining study.

Heart

It is one thing to confront bodily suffering and to push into unknown mental territory, but suffering of the heart is a different matter. The lover scorned, the business associate betrayed, the child unloved, and the soldier left behind all experience suffering wished on no one. However, suffering of the heart gets at the root of true meaning. There is a reason Dante's lowest level of hell is for betrayers. Placing your heart on the line is a daunting task. Hence why past slights and hurts manifest later in life. It happens to the abused woman struggling to be open with her spouse, the fatherless child avoiding the responsibilities of fatherhood, or the bullied kid lashing out. Suffering of the heart cuts deep.

Regardless of the cut, confronting suffering often reveals what is meaningful. As many parents know, some of the greatest meaning is found in raising children. Happily married couples attest to this on their fiftieth wedding anniversary after making it through sickness, health, riches, poverty, and everything in between. Is it easy? Nope. Worth it? You better believe it.

To start, put your heart out there. Having a strong and conditioned (note: *not* hardened) heart helps find meaning.

The fear of public speaking is most people's greatest fear. Why? It risks the heart. When you speak publicly, it means you risk judgment by your community, your peers, and typically the people closest to you.

The graveyard is the richest place on earth. There, you find unfulfilled hopes and dreams, unwritten books, unsung songs, unshared inventions, and undiscovered cures. All because someone was too afraid to take that first step (Les Brown).

It is one thing to risk judgment, but you must take responsibility for that judgment. Athletes understand this, as they enter competition to be judged. If they blame the judges, we call them "poor sports." It cuts more deeply in real life, where you must take responsibility for your children, spouse, friendships, and communities. A spouse may judge you as inadequate and leave. That creates heart suffering. Taking responsibility for your perceived inadequacy induces a deeper pain.

You want to be loved for who you are, but you are inadequate, fallen, broken, and misled. Any spouse, business partner, or friend can leave for many justifiable reasons. Take responsibility for this. It is your responsibility to confront illusions and lies in your life and to work toward becoming more. You are not a mere animal trapped by your nature! You can become more if you take responsibility for change, but you must admit this about yourself—and that is difficult. You do not need a therapist encouraging you to accept yourself. You need a confessional where you admit your failings and turn from them.

An important aside here—we are all inadequate in a multitude of ways, just as judges (of any sort) take responsibility for the inadequacies of their judgments. Take the example of athletes blaming a judge or referee for the outcome of a competition. Athletes should never leave the outcome in the hands of the judge; they should take responsibility for the outcome themselves. Take responsibility for your inadequacies, but don't stop there. Take responsibility for everyone else's inadequacies, just as others take responsibility for yours.

The athlete who does not finish the competition with enough margin places the judge in an unfair place where imperfect judgments lead to imperfect results. Because we are all inadequate, we constantly place others in unfair positions where their inadequacies emerge. In the same way, others will place us in positions where we act, speak, feel, and think in inadequate ways.

The only option is to position ourselves in a way that others' inadequacies cannot harm us when (because of our own inadequacies) we cannot resolve an issue. It is complicated but necessary. We will revisit this in more detail and by example in chapter 3.

The first step in taking responsibility for the heart is to take responsibility for your feelings. In my observation, males and females approach this differently, but each are responsible for their feelings.

The second step is to admit and address your feelings. This is often where men and women differ. Women typically address their feelings outwardly, through conversation. Men, on the other hand, typically address feelings inwardly through self-reflection. These are not absolutes, but they are common enough traits to be helpful.

Step three: you must act. Men fail at this step when they bury emotion. Women fail by bringing the emotion into the light but leaving it unresolved. These are actions, but neither is beneficial. Unresolved or buried emotions fester, causing suffering on the surface or deep inside.

Action must be taken in a way to resolve emotion. Ultimately, self-control (physical, mental, emotional, and spiritual) is mastery of the self. You do not want to bounce from highs to lows. This can indicate addiction. Happiness and joy are wonderful. Seeking the highs of extremely good emotions is as dangerous as wallowing in the depths of despair. Action to resolve emotion should correlate with the emotion. Ask yourself what you are doing or allowing to foster the emotional situation. Emotions are natural signals your brain provides for a reason. Be aware of them and act to guard against emotional extremes that foment a loss of control.

The goal is contentment. You achieve this by putting other's contentment ahead of your own, addressing your lack of contentment, and dealing with your own inadequacies that diminish contentment. This is a complex dichotomy. When you meet a stranger, you want to be accepted. Push too hard and you come across as overbearing; stay silent and inactive, and you come across as uncaring. Balance these drives with natural contentment, accepting yourself and the judgments of others.

One of the best places to develop emotional control is with service to others. This is emotional action. However, it must be unforced. Any type of force, guilt, or responsibility (such as a job or court order, parental force or mandated public service) negates the emotional effort. Helping a widow, volunteering, caring for children, and working in a soup kitchen reap internal benefits when performed out of a desire from the heart.

People who are naturally empathetic and do not have well-guarded emotions can get taken advantage of in these situations. Instead of learning to manage emotions, you can swing from negative emotions to seeking self-worth from others. Remember—service to others is good, but self-worth never comes from others.

Working under supervision with a group or official organization is best. Also, be cautious of helping others in your same situation. One addict helping another without support can have disastrous results. You need some distance from addiction before you can help another in the same situation. Group settings and accountability partners are healthy ways to deal with such issues.

The other side of the coin is risk. Putting others' contentment ahead of your own means putting your own being on the line. You can learn to be empathic. You can also learn to protect yourself emotionally at the same time. Go home from the hospice center, finish the youth softball practice, and leave the emotions at the place of service.

The next evolution of this is when you risk your being (what makes you unique and original) to please another. This is the stage-fright scenario. An actor or actress (in both a real and metaphorical sense) speaks out with a unique frame of reference to provide contentment to others and puts their being and inadequacies on the line. The greatest art risks the artist's heart because it risks the inadequacies of being. It risks betrayal and being judged by those whose opinions they value. The more an artist risks their being and listens to the judges, takes responsibility for these actions, and reincorporates feedback into their being, the greater the work.

This is not just art—it is life. It is every relationship, every business, every career, every marriage, and every community. What is the heart of your being? What is all of you? Take all of self (body, mind, heart, and spirit), skills, relationships, environment, resources, and purpose. Then risk it all in being judged! It will always be inadequate. Own it. This is painful, but you are growing and drawing closer to the spirit of the matter.

Spirit

We live in an age of modernity, where tangible matter and science dominate culture. This was not the case for most of written history. In the recent past, people concerned themselves with the spirit as much as, if not more than, the physical. This concern with the spiritual eventually led to luxury sufficient for indulging in scientific undertakings.

Because spirit is not physically tangible, there is a challenge describing it within the constraints of a physical world. The spirit is substance and energy and has describable characteristics. Some describe spirit as *heart* (often they use the word *soul*). Without a doubt, the spirit interacts with your emotional self. However, it is more than just your heart.

> The word of God is living and active and sharper than any two-edged sword—piercing right through to a separation of soul and spirit, joints and marrow, and able to judge the thoughts and intentions of the heart. (Hebrews 4:12 TLV)

Modern science has proved that Bible verse correct. Science shows the brain's biochemistry (dopamine, norepinephrine, and serotonin) significantly influences your emotions. Emotions, your heart or soul, are not as mysterious as once thought and are substantially under your control. Your spirit is something different.

Some describe spirit as the essence of the mind, the amalgamation of your thoughts and feelings. Some describe spirit as a mystical force interacting with the physical. Some describe spirit as being outside of yourself, a thing of the divine.

The divine is spirit, yet in all religions, the divine interacts with and through the physical as an emotional being with a mind. If it were not so, you could not perceive the divine. Logically, whatever is more than physical is over the physical. The spirit proceeds from the divine, as with the physical.

Wildly, science and mathematics have speculated and proven additional dimensions. Edwin Abbott's 1884 novella *Flatland* tells us about "A Square," a two-dimensional being. This character comes to believe in a third dimension of cubes and spheres and in a fourth and beyond of hypercubes and hyper-hypercubes (Wikipedia: Flatland 2019). In 1920, Albert Einstein predicted a fourth dimension. Scientist Carl Sagan explained this theory, referencing *Flatland* on his television show, *Cosmos*. More recently, proof of the fourth dimension has emerged (see Zilberberg et al. 2018). Yet it remains difficult to speak to what the physical, mental, and emotional components of a divine being beyond our universe or dimension would be.

I believe your spirit is as unique and individual as your body, mind, and heart. From it flows character, will, life, and essence. It allows you to combine, compute, and abstract stories and symbols beyond what you sense. Your physical, mental, and emotional self is an imperfect reflection and is only temporarily in this dimension.

Your spirit powers action, emotion, and thought—it is the spark of a creator. You must be careful here. Lean into the spirit of the truth and not the spirit of lies. What you create with your writing, art, music, and equations reflects the spirit of self or a higher spirit. Therefore, your spirit is essential. Its primacy can be hard to see in suffering. This is one reason mastering suffering is helpful. It allows you to overcome unnatural and resistive parts of yourself and focus on the spiritual. However, a developed spiritual self can overcome physical, mental, or emotional roadblocks. The lives of the saints testify to this.

There is a dichotomy to consider. Suffering physically, mentally, or emotionally can awaken a hope for something more. Jesus told Nicodemus that regardless of how far you develop spiritually, a person born of the flesh cannot fully partake of the Spirit until born of the Spirit. Lean into that which stirs a desire for the spiritual, remembering that the truly spiritual transcends your individual spirit. If you are not guided by the Holy Spirit, you risk pursuing a false spirituality.

The spiritual is not tied to time. What is most infused with the spirit lasts longer than those of body, mind, and heart. The most spiritual things always outlast their physical, mental, or emotional counterparts. This is the Lindy effect at work.

The spirit is a great mystery. The more you understand, the more you realize how far you have to go. Part of you is connected to those other dimensions. The choices you make have more consequence than you realize. What are the consequences of building a selfish, dishonest, lazy, and inadequate self? What are the consequences of grabbing power in this dimension? For the Christian, letting go of the self, accepting the cross, and placing God ahead of self is the only way to mitigate the ultimate danger of pride.

This world is more than physical, and science does not teach how to live. The value of a painting is not in the amount of paper and paint that was used. Science can measure a sphere, describe it, and discuss its volume and weight. Science cannot, however, explain what the item means to you. Is it a ball for playing catch and building relationships, a globe for explaining and mapping the world, or a weapon to hurl at an enemy out of anger? If science cannot tell what to do with a sphere, it certainly can't give meaning to a hypercube.

Seek to live a purposeful life. Seek what is meaningful. Confront the suffering of your spirit. In biblical terminology, "The fruits of the Spirit are good." Building qualities of love, joy, and peace is important, so foster these qualities. They empower you to confront suffering and transcend your physical, mental, and emotional situation.

Out of love, a parent will brave great danger for their child. A soldier will give up their life for peace. Those who take joy in facing obstacles will overcome them. Look for characteristics that transcend the mind, heart, and body, and foster the good ones.

Next, confront spiritual suffering by putting away lustful thoughts, not overeating, giving away everything you have, not oversleeping, focusing on making the world better, not getting angry, and envying no one. Do this in secret. If you do, you will fully integrate what psychiatrist Carl Jung dubbed the "shadow self."

Your dark, sinful nature is where suffering multiplies and manifests in action, thought, and feeling. Confronting your "shadow self" or your sin nature is hard, because you like to hide it. In fact, confronting spiritual suffering seems impossible! You are inadequate to the task, and when it shows, you feel guilty. You yell at someone, tell a lie, overindulge, sleep in, burn with jealousy, look down your nose at others, covet, or gossip and betray. Embarrassed by these parts of yourself, you avoid dealing with them. I do the same, but there is a way through these failures.

The way of the cross moves you past these shortcomings. Jesus took upon himself the shortcomings of humankind—the guilt for lust, gluttony, greed, laziness, wrath, jealousy, pride, and betrayal. At the same time, Jesus was without sin, bearing and cultivating all fruits of the Spirit. Following him to the cross resolves your shortcomings.

Let me be clear: you do not want to possess your dark side. It can easily possess. Recognize those traits, accept them, and confront them. This is the essence of Reinhold Niebuhr's famous "Serenity Prayer":

God, grant me the serenity to accept the things I cannot change,
Courage to change the things I can,
And wisdom to know the difference.

What evil are you capable of carrying out? Could you kill, betray, or worse? Those are extremes, but could you lie, gossip, judge another person, or be jealous?

"Yes, but I would never . . ."

How little would your situation have to change for you to lie, envy, steal, or kill? Aleksandr Solzhenitsyn considered this in *The Gulag Archipelago*. He wrote, "The line dividing good and evil cuts through the heart of every human being." Turn on the news and see this in today's genocides, child sacrifices, theft, coercion, tyrannical actions, and worldly theories. I see it in myself and ignore it. Do you?

Assess your faults. Don't dwell on them and have a pity party, but plan how to overcome them. Then let go of them to emulate a higher way of being, to follow a better example, and to walk a new path!

Start viewing yourself as a victimizer. Take control of yourself, including that darker nature. You grow and learn when you confront your imperfections. In the Christian walk, this takes form in confession and trusting the Spirit to make all things work out for good.

Take something of your dark characteristics and use it for good. If you're an angry person, turn that energy into something positive. If you're lazy, look for a new challenge. Feel you are a good person already? Get to know yourself better. And ask others how you can grow.

Another way to confront spirit suffering is dialogue. Religions and communities like Alcoholic Anonymous know the power of talking. We are all repressing something. Confront the suffering of your spirit openly with others by confessing your suffering. Others can often see what you are repressing and help you understand it. By doing this, they can give you perspective.

Following the lives of others who confront spiritual suffering can teach you how to live. Of these, none is better than Jesus of Nazareth. Read the early church fathers, saints, the Puritans, and—one of my favorites—Captain Ernest Gordon. They teach how to face suffering. Apply this to spiritual, physical, mental, and emotional arenas. Many secular greats followed the lives of others. Alexander wanting to be like Achilles and Scipio emulated Cyrus.

So, who are you following?

Chapter 3

RELATIONSHIPS

He who knows others is wise; he who knows himself is enlightened.
—Lao Tzu

If civilization is to survive, we must cultivate the science of human relationships—the ability of all peoples, of all kinds, to live together, in the same world at peace.
—Franklin D. Roosevelt

Types of Relationships

Relationships are important, and you should understand them clearly. We are all individuals. Because we are individuals, we are at different places along our journeys. These differences create complications. Understanding how to relate to others in different places can minimize these complications.

There are three types of relationships involving teacher, student, and partner. A parent-child relationship is an extreme example of a teacher-student relationship. A boss and employee can have a teacher-student relationship. However, a boss and employee relationship can be a partnership. Or it can be a student-teacher relationship if the boss hires the employee to fulfill needs in an area in which the boss lacks! Do not be overly rigid in relationship dichotomies and structures.

A teacher understands and knows, has experienced, learned, felt, done, or moved along the path in a narrow field or characteristic. We all should be teachers of something.

A student is a seeker along a path looking for experience or knowledge. It is helpful for students to learn from others, as trial and error is time-consuming and difficult. That said, students cannot wait for the right teacher. They often find the teacher after beginning the path, as the teacher is often a fellow traveler.

Partners are spouse, business, sibling, and other peers. Partnerships are relationships between peers on an equal footing. Individuals can be on different parts of the path, but they are not teachers. The best partnerships occur when both partners walk similar paths in unique ways. You see this in business when an introverted engineer builds an amazing product, and an extroverted salesperson markets the product. In marriage, male and female try to be the best man and woman they can. Partnerships are most effective when the partners trust the other's strengths and cover for each other's weaknesses.

In relationships, it is advisable to never assume the teacher's role. Not everybody is looking for a teacher, especially your spouse or business partner. They may respect your strengths but have no desire to emulate them. Because the teacher has influence over the student, a student who decides to teach the teacher plays against an ego that may or may not be self-actualized. You risk losing the teacher by trying to teach them.

The default role to live in is that of a student. Come to relationship hungry to walk the path. There is no obtainable destination; being is always becoming. Darth Vader told Ben Kenobi, "I am the master. Your powers are weak, old man." But Vader was not the master—Obi-Wan "Ben" Kenobi was. Vader struck down Kenobi, but Kenobi vanished. Kenobi remained on his path of becoming and took a step into the spiritual realm, where he wielded more influence and power.

The Key Traits

Navigating relationships begins in the heart. Your heart drives your emotions and is classically called the *soul*. In recent history, it has been identified as producing chemical reactions within your brain and creating feelings of joy, fear, sadness, and love.

A 2014 Harvard paper states, "Many psychological scientists now assume that emotions are the dominant driver of most meaningful decisions in life" (Lerner 2014). Salespeople learn that people purchase items based on emotions and justify the purchases logically. It is safe to conclude that you build the strongest relationships around emotional connections.

Having physical, intellectual, and spiritual relationships can be beneficial. Your work requires intellect, your favorite sport demands specific physical traits, and significant relationships have a spiritual component. Championship teams play other teams with the same number of players, similar physical abilities, and similar understanding of the sport. Yet there can be tremendous differences in outcomes, even at the highest levels, because relationships are stronger than the sum of parts.

Relationships aligned along physical, mental, emotional, and spiritual lines are stronger; people in these relationships know they are engaged in something bigger than themselves. This is true of all healthy personal relationships, businesses, and communities.

Still, the most meaningful relationships connect at a heart level. This connection takes place at different places for different people because individuals have their hearts in all kinds of places. Take responsibility to identify the heart of those with whom you have relationships.

Good salespeople know to do this. They find what the other person cares about and sell accordingly. A good salesperson sells the safest tires, best rated insurance policy, and most spacious home to the client who values family. Conversely, the good salesperson will sell the same products in different ways to different people. For example, selling name-brand tires, insurance plan with the strength of a strong financial institution, or a house that will turn the most heads to someone who cares about prestige and personal identity. Identifying people's hearts is a powerful key to navigating relationships. It is the root of empathy.

Some relationships do not require this. The clerk at the grocery store does not require an emotional relationship to process the grocery transaction. However, as you develop empathy, you will realize and read others' emotions. You can offer words of encouragement or give a smile to soften the weight of a hard day on a slumping clerk. Of course, these actions run the risk of rejection. Yet this potential rejection is seldom realized. Instead, your kindness is received and helps improve the world.

To develop and strengthen your empathic nature, observe people. If you are an introvert, it will feel unnatural and can lead to interactions with strangers. That's okay! Without staring at people, observe how they move through the world. Are they in a hurry, sad, angry, happy, carefree? If you are naturally empathetic, experiencing others' emotions can be a roller coaster ride. If you are extroverted and driven, you may struggle to identify emotions, and it will take practice to do it accurately.

Eye contact is an important trait to develop. One of humanity's deepest desires is to be seen. We want to be seen in our happy moments. We want others to enjoy our triumphs and celebrations. The popularity of Facebook illustrates this desire. People post their perfect meals, vacations, and children. But this only tells part of the story. We also want to be seen in our pain and suffering. We may not post it online, but there is a deep desire to be seen in our pain. It's why sad songs become popular. We gain solace knowing somebody else understands our emotional situation.

We fall in love with a character when an author captures our feelings of romance, adventure, pain, or joy. We want to be seen.

We tend to shy away from eye contact with a crying person. You suspect they do not want you to see them like this, but in reality, you want to avoid feeling their pain. It is the simple way out.

The most tragic outcome comes when people have their pain and suffering avoided for a lifetime. This can occur when parents offer no comfort or conversely coddle children to protect them from pain. Later in life, pain causes them to withdraw or lash out even more. Friends, boyfriends, girlfriends, and spouses are less likely to see their pain or pursue seeing them in their pain. This problem can multiply when one believes that showing emotional pain is unhealthy.

Hidden pain leads to broken hearts, divorce, loneliness, suicide, and more. You cannot cut yourself off from humanity. You need others to see you, and you need to see others!

The lesson is simple—do not avoid eye contact— no longer than three seconds is needed (Jarrett 2016). Make eye contact when talking, when a person is sad, when greeting and leaving. See the people around you. You will feel a part of their pain, happiness, or other emotion. Authentically, you will share their burdens and joys. This lessens burdens and spreads joy. Just as infants prefer and process faces that gaze at them (Jarrett 2016), so you will develop deeper relationships.

Along with eye contact, be conscientious of body language. A soft smile made with eye contact can go a long way to ease pain.

Body language says a lot about a person. The military starts with it—Attention! March! Proper posture communicates competence and courage. A leader can turn up pressure on an employee and see if their posture breaks, eyes look away, and speech patterns change. Body language draws in or pushes out. Be conscious of your body language and what it says. Good posture, a warm attitude, leaning toward the other person, and the maintaining uncrossed arms go a long way.

Speech is important as well. You may think the words you speak are most important, but this is incorrect. A 1967 study by Albert Mehrabian showed that the actual words used can be less important than eye contact, body language, tone, and tempo. Body language accounts for 55 percent, tone for 38 percent, and words for 7 percent. When I say *speech*, I am referring to tone and tempo. Listen to "Hook" by Blues Traveler, a song sung with great inflection. Many speakers and preachers use tone and tempo to draw you in while saying nothing!

Any sentence can change meaning by changing your tone and tempo. Example: "I love you." Spoken slowly and without emphasis, "I love you" sounds bored, flat, and almost meaningless—a lie. Spoken fast, emphasizing every word—"I love you"—is a chore, something forced, probably a lie. Emphasize the first word and you turn the sentence into something selfish. Emphasize *love* and the sentence becomes about the emotion or feeling. Emphasize the last word and the sentence focuses on the person receiving the love. Yes, it is that easy to miscommunicate.

Another aspect of tone is emotion. "How may I help you?" sounds different when spoken through a smile or frown. Don't believe it? Turn your back to and friend and ask if you can help them. Say it first while frowning and then smiling. Ask which was said with a smile. They can probably guess.

As for tempo, speed the sentence up and it feels rushed; slow it down and you sound bored. Consider the monotonous teacher compared to the passionate teacher. Typically, you learn more from the passionate teacher. Yet passion looks different in different settings. In the United States, Southerners and hillbillies like me have famously slower speech patterns that accent their Southern drawl. Talk fast to them and they'll feel you don't care about whatever you're saying. Others have the opposite reaction. Speak slowly to Northerners, and they feel you are wasting their time. Want to avoid both ditches? Mirror the speech pattern of those around you and be conscious of what meaning you want to impart.

Finally, grammar is important. It helps ensure clarity and effective communication of your ideas. At a foundational level, it communicates that you care about what you are saying. The poor primary educational system in the United States has led to more people with poor grammar; always seek to better yourself without judging others.

This section barely scratches the surface. Strive to empathize with and to care about others. Show it in your eyes, body language, tone, tempo, and words. The pinnacle of successful communication is honesty. Communication is one of the most powerful human abilities. The ability to tell and believe stories separated us from our ancestors (Homo erectus) and allowed us to reshape the world. As with anything powerful, it is easy to abuse. Skilled communicators can manipulate. Governments, organizations, and powerful people throughout time have harnessed this power. Hitler and Churchill are examples of the power of communication, manipulation, and media control. Do not neglect the power of communication in your life and on your life.

A transcendent trait of good communication is listening. As Stephen Covey puts it, "Seek first to understand, then to be understood." Politicians are excellent with body language, eye contact, tone, and tempo—they make you believe they know what they are saying. Listen to their words and you'll realize they rarely know what they are talking about! Watch their actions, too. This can be hard. Whether it is a politician you support or don't support, you naturally hear what you want to hear, a phenomenon known as confirmation bias.

Pleasurable, quality, confirmation bias noise causes you to not listen. This noise, both in quantity and quality, is increasing. No wonder nearly half of all marriages end in divorce. The leading cause of divorce is a failure to listen. In fact, the most powerful form of communication is silence. However, if you go silent in a marriage, it is because the other party is not listening. If the other spouse were engaged and listening, the silence would not stand.

If you listen, you can mirror other people better and create a stronger connection. You will feel their pains and joys and share in them.

Listen with your body—make eye contact, lean forward, draw close, and open your arms. Listen with your mind to hear what they are saying, what they are not saying, how are they saying it, and why. Listen with your heart to what they feel and do not feel. Finally, listen with the spirit to grasp what their subconscious is communicating.

Good listeners perceive subconscious communication, which presents itself in small incongruities between the body, mind, and heart. Consider the confident speaker who speaks clearly, concisely, and passionately but whose hands are fidgety or shaking. Fear, dishonesty, or something else is at play. Incongruities do not always mean something sinister, but they do mean something.

Good listening is taking responsibility for the words of another. It allows you to confront suffering and create meaning. What happens if you find pain, sorrow, and hopelessness? If you are truly listening, you feel (physically, mentally, emotionally, and spiritually) what they are communicating. This release of emotional chemicals enhances your learning process.

> If I were to summarize in one sentence the single most important principle I have learned in the field of interpersonal relations, it would be this: Seek first to understand, then to be understood. (Stephen R. Covey)

Partnerships

Relationships are easier if you have yourself figured out. If you don't master yourself, you enter relationships on imperfect terms. Every relationship has a share of challenge and suffering. However, there are a couple of things to do before entering a personal or professional partnership relationship.

Make the partnership as equal as possible. Neither partner should have an advantage or disadvantage in the relationship. This is important, but it is also impossible. You have your own unique situation and are your own unique person; the same is true for your partner. Therefore, balance is hard to achieve and harder to maintain. Yet somehow, relationships work.

How does the ugly guy end up with the beautiful wife? There is often a balance elsewhere—he is funny, rich, intelligent, spiritual, or skilled at showing love. The problem arises when the balance is missed and the funny guy gets the beautiful girl. If the funny guy puts on a show to get the girl, there will be an imbalance when he tires of the act. She will realize he is not funny after a hard day at work. He is not funny after being up all night with a newborn. Now we have a problem. The reverse can be true too. He is always funny, and she gets annoyed. She is always beautiful, and he gets jealous. These situations occur when two people enter a balanced relationship but do not understand or recognize this balance. At the start, the couple may recognize the balance, but forget about it or take it for granted over time.

The same occurs in professional relationships. One person provides financing up front, and the other brings "sweat equity" to the table. All is well at the start. But what happens after a year, two, or ten? Without considering the need and purpose of balance, things fall apart.

For these reasons, the better you know yourself the better you will maintain balance. Be honest upfront. Recognize your weaknesses. Make the other person aware of them. Being honest about your faults does not mean you are seeking the other person's help to overcome those faults—that person is not your teacher. If you share faults in order to get help or support, the partnership relationship fails. It transitions from a partnership to a parent-child, teacher-student, or boss-employee relationship. This is a difficult transition that often spells the end.

This often happens when a female vents to a male and doesn't want the male to solve the problem. Men should listen better—it is not his job to solve his partner's problem. Conversely, women should do the same—listen, not to what a man says but to what he does. Men may not talk about their problems, but they are having them. Acting tired, deep in thought, and emotionally withdrawn may mean a man is processing and dealing with difficult problems. A woman who listens with more than her ears creates a quiet, controlled environment conducive for men to work through issues. Men often get labeled as terrible listeners (often warranted), but women can be the same. Women want their words to be heard; men want their actions heard. A listening woman respects a man's silence. A listening woman creates a space in which her partner can process problems internally.

The best partnership is balanced. Both parties listen to each other (physically, mentally, emotionally, and spiritually) and take responsibility for their own weaknesses and shortcomings, using their strengths to benefit the partnership.

If you have entered a partnership with imbalance, unshared vision, or poor communication, remember chapter 1. Suffering happens. No relationship is perfect, and meaning resides in confronting challenges to become the best person possible. My wife always says, "The key to a successful marriage is to never fall out of love at the same time." There are always times and places where you can blame another. In your situation, 99 percent of the blame may belong to your partner, but you still share responsibility.

If your partner is not listening, it is your fault. When a movie flops at the box office, is it the audience's fault or the moviemakers'? Moviemakers may say the audience was too stupid to get it. They're wrong, and they just alienated their prime audience. Blame your partner, and you do the same thing. There will always be communication challenges and imbalances. Work through them without blame or excuses.

Have a partner who does not listen? Maybe you are the problem. Perhaps you do a poor job of communicating. People are poor listeners, and you cannot control them. You can, however, communicate and listen better.

First, listen to the full person. Second, communicate with the full person. Do actions, attitudes, and spirit not match words spoken? When a husband says, "I love you," while he works late nights, does not help around the house, never brings flowers, and ogles bikini-clad ladies at the beach, his words ring hollow. The employee who says, "I care about my job," but is late, does shoddy work, has a poor attitude, and takes excessive time off may not care about their job.

In some cases, the opposite occurs, leaving the wife confused. "My husband never says 'I love you,'" she thinks. However, he gets home at a decent hour, helps with the kids, and cooks dinner occasionally. All the bills stay paid and he falls asleep early at night from a long day. Despite this, the wife remains frustrated because he never says he loves her. Is she listening fully to her husband? Probably not. Could the man do better? Of course!

Some people "hear" better along certain characteristics, and you can communicate better and easier if you know "where" the other party listens best. If they look for words you do not give, you fall short. Just remember that words can be manipulative. Constant words of love and assurance not followed up with actions, heart, and spirit may not mean much. The emotional bank account will realize it is full of IOUs (Covey 1989). Communicate fully in a language your partner understands.

Imbalances are best communicated with openness and transparency. Identify the imbalance and clearly communicate your intention to make up the discrepancy elsewhere. This is easier in a quantifiable situation, such as a business partnership. It is harder in a personal relationship. Honesty and transparency about how the partnership will work on the front end are best. Honesty and transparency when imbalances are uncovered are crucial.

If you are not equal to your partner, focus on your strength and being the best you can in the relationship. Build other aspects of being without your partner's help. Communicate this with your partner clearly, without asking for help. Instead, communicate a humble desire to serve the partner by growing into a fuller, self-actualized person. The solution is always for the person on the negative side of the imbalance to step up their game.

If your partner is growing, the worst thing to do is to hamper that growth. Your partner's growth is a benefit to all, yourself included. Do everything in your power to encourage and support your partner's growth, then get to growing yourself.

Since you are reading this book, you may have the opposite issue. You are growing but your partner is stagnant. In business, this is often seen in sales, hours worked, objectives accomplished, etc. In personal relationships, it can be less quantifiable. This is a good thing. And who cares if your partner is stagnant?

You are not in control of others, but only yourself. Besides, you are not growing if you are busy criticizing others! If your business partner is lazy, take the opportunity to guide the ship. Your spouse is boring and predictable. Good! It's easier to know how to show them love. Instead of judging, treat them like they're growing. Most likely, your partner is doing just that in ways you cannot perceive because you are different.

Unfortunately, partners can grow apart. Saving the partnership requires you to grow toward the other. By communicating vision and purpose for the future, you can keep the growth aligned.

Of course, growing faster than your partner is usually fine. The stronger can carry the relationship through hard times. You may be strong today, but that can change. Pride and arrogance come before the fall. So do your best to "outgrow" your partner. Just remember not to compare yourself to others, especially your partner. Do you really want another person who looks, thinks, and acts just like you?

A word on abuse. Abuse can happen when the "weak" feed off the "strong" or the "strong" dominate the "weak." It happens if you think you have truly "outgrown" your partner. You may look at them as "less than" or feel your partner owes you. Physical and psychological abuse easily follow in personal relationships. In professional relationships, theft and betrayal may arise.

Do you put your head in the sand and take the abuse. This is not suffering. Confronting suffering requires you to speak up and act to stop abuse. Avoid personal retaliation, but do not allow criminal offense and injustice to take place.

> [Love] does not dishonor others, it is not self-seeking, it is not easily angered, it keeps no record of wrongs. . . . It always protects.
> (1 Corinthians 13:5, 7 NIV)

Chapter 4

COMMUNITY

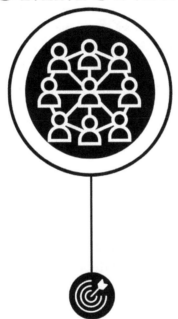

Adopt responsibility for your own well-being, try to put your family together, try to serve your community, try to seek for eternal truth. . . . That's the sort of thing that can ground you in your life, enough so that you can withstand the difficulty of life.

—Jordan Peterson

The purpose of life is to discover your gift.
The work of life is to develop it.
The meaning of life is to give your gift away.

—David Viscott

Back to the Individual

If purpose is best discovered in confronting suffering and bringing peace, best relationships are those in which we are students, and the healthiest partnership includes balanced listening and serving, then the healthiest communities encourage and allow these behaviors.

I use *community* in a broad sense to include local communities such as towns and large communities like nations. Your church, business, or other organization are communities too. As is your family unit.

You make communities of individuals and individual relationships. When a community stops serving individuals to focus on groups, a problem arises, particularly if the individual cannot escape the community. This is dire when the government (i.e. leadership of a community) is for or against a group of people. Taxation, representation, benefits, and services not equally distributed is wrong. Return to the section on relationships and partnerships—the goal is balance. Remember how easily personal relationships become unbalanced. Multiply this by government systems, and you see how one group becomes terrorized by another. This develops history's tyrants, socialist ideology, and ultranationalism: one group is oppressed by another, those in power oppress the powerless, the poor rob the rich, the rich rob the poor, the ultranational rob the non-ultranational, and the educated dupe the uneducated. Revolution must take place (ideally at ballot boxes and in public and private conversations) when government thinks it knows better than you.

Smaller communities also need to exist to allow the individual to have a vehicle in which to grow. A business with the right people moves in the right direction. In Jim Collins's study of over a thousand good companies, going from good to great did not happen in companies that focused on vision, mission, and strategy first. The companies that focused on getting the right people first became great (Collins 2001).

Churches that develop their people ("make disciples") have stronger congregations! People often think that Jesus's Great Commission is about going to the world and converting people to Christianity. That is the easy part. The full commission is to make disciples—much harder! Read these words of Jesus:

"Therefore, go and *make disciples of all nations*, baptizing them in the name of the Father and of the Son and of the Holy Spirit, and teaching them to obey everything I have commanded you. And surely I am with you always, to the very end of the age." (Mathew 28:19–20 NIV, emphasis added)

People who are empowered to grow physically, mentally, emotionally, and spiritually will grow. Then, they will serve. What kind of customer service does an oppressed, belittled, underpaid customer service rep deliver? None.

Direction, vision, or mission of a community can aim outward toward others, bringing others into the community of growth. However, individuals within the community must grow first. If not, they will have nothing to offer.

I have served as a financial adviser, accountant, consultant, and financial officer most of my life. The greatest tragedy of modern accounting systems is seeing payroll as an expense instead of an investment. Viewing payroll as an expense is antiquated and ineffective. That most generally accepted accounting principles (GAAP), tax laws, and regulations do not update this is testimony to the general stupidity of financial people, including myself. Employees are valuable assets that can appreciate instead of depreciate! Alas, rewriting a vast chunk of GAAP is beyond this book. This shortfall in accepted accounting principles contains a powerful advantage for those who realize it and can use it in their community.

Invest

A community should treat people as investments and invest in their physical, mental, emotional, and spiritual health. Unfortunately, it rarely happens.

Schools teach math, science, writing, reading, and a little physical education. Yet our schools invest little in emotional training, relationship guidance, art, music, philosophy, and spiritual training.

We as parents do a poor job investing as well. Do we model healthy eating? The obesity epidemic statistics show we do not. Do we model good relationships and emotional health? Not when we look at our hours spent consuming TV and Facebook. Do we model spiritual growth? Polls tracking religion, meaning and purpose, church attendance, and understanding the metaphysical world makes it clear that we do not. This does not bode well for future generations.

It would help ease suffering if we confronted it and encouraged others to do the same. Begin building yourself into whom you could be. Make yourself the example your community needs. You will not influence people by being weak, stupid, emotionally unstable, and without spirit. Start improving yourself and then worry about the relationships closest to you—those with your spouse, children, and business partners. If you are on the path, invest in those around you. Encourage them. Help them. But start with you.

Why? Living a meaningful life is hard. Many people will outright refuse. If you are not secure in yourself, you cannot take the emotional strain of sharing this message with others. Worse, you will listen to people who want to keep you down. They will say you are good just the way you are, and that you should accept yourself and not be judgmental.

Focus on being a better person and making healthier relationships. When you do, people will listen, and some will follow. As you excel you will get raises and promotions at work, your town and church will ask your opinion, and you may find yourself in a place of leadership. Then the real challenge starts! Because in that position, when you stumble and fall, it will be in front of many. "Better to die than never truly live!"

If you gain success and a following, you may forget what put you in that position. Instead of focusing on challenging yourself, your goal weakens to maintaining your position or prestige earned by past actions.

Why do revival preachers preach on a circuit? The church rarely wants to hear the painful message too often! Why do politicians promise the world but never deliver? It is the only way they can get elected. Why do so many businesses under-deliver on their value propositions? It is easy to lose purpose and meaning when surrounded by success and the "easy" life. Do not lose yourself in "success," because ultimately there is no such thing.

Make sure you are not made "Emperor." Avoid that imperial stain. It can happen to you, so keep yourself simple, good, pure, saintly, plain, a friend of justice, god-fearing, gracious, affectionate, and strong for your proper work. Fight to remain the person that philosophy wished to make you. Revere the gods, and look after each other. Life is short—the fruit of this life is a good character and acts for the common good. (Marcus Aurelius)

If you are in a position of leadership and not fully living a purposeful life, do not worry about applying these principles to serving the community. Most likely, you are not capable—individual self must come first. However, if you are growing spiritually and living a meaningful, healthy, focused, mentally developed, and emotionally secure life with healthy personal relationships, it is time for true suffering to begin. Put yourself out there—at work, at church, in your town, for your nation and for all of humanity. Start small—in your home, work, or church. Write a book, give back, and invest in the people closest to you.

Start Small

If you have your life in order, apply these principles in your home, at your work, within an organization, or in your local community.

Through suffering and challenge, you grow and become better. Apply this at work. Do your job, whether it requires physical, mental, emotional, or spiritual work.

You can complete your job by doing the bare minimum. However, if you aim at a meaningful life, such an approach to work is inconsistent. Go beyond the minimum and work with purpose. It is harder, more painful, and more meaningful.

If your job is primarily mental, emotional, or spiritual, then you must also bring physical energy to your work. You must exercise if your work has limited physicality. It is physically undemanding to sit behind a desk, stand behind a pulpit, or sit across from another as you talk, think, write, figure, or engage in emotional, mental, or spiritual ways. However, if you lack energy or experience other problems stemming from a lack of physical exertion, you only go through the motions of mind, heart, or spirit.

New research has uncovered how deadly sitting behind a desk is for the human body. With an estimate 80 percent of the US population engaging in desk-based work, this is bad news! The US National Library of Medicine (MedlinePlus 2018) lists the following dangers of a sedentary lifestyle: slow metabolism, increased weight, less muscle and endurance, weaker bones, compromised immune system, slower blood circulation, increased inflammation, hormonal imbalance, and increased risk of disease, stroke, metabolic syndrome, diabetes, cancer, osteoporosis, and feelings of depression and anxiety.

If your body is your engine, what type of drive can you truly have in your nonphysical job if you're using a go-cart engine? Nonphysical work can be more stressful and draining than physical work, as you deal with other people, their emotions and problems. The nature of dealing with situations and circumstances outside of your control adds to the stress. This is another critical reason for exercise. The more mentally, emotionally, and spiritually demanding your work, the harder you should exercise. Get a standing desk, move around your job space, and start exercising—no exceptions.

If your job is not mentally demanding, take time to engage with and think about what it is you do—physically, emotionally, or spiritually. (Review chapter 2, subsection "Mind.") Remember the three ways to develop the mind: pray, study, and create. Apply this to what you do! Think about what is getting done, study how others get it done, and then test and create new ways of getting it done. Do not worry about big changes. Strive after minor, one-percent improvements. They add up. Do this for the job you do, make mistakes, and learn. Can you do the work one percent cheaper, faster, or better, or are there physical improvements you can make? Can you connect with individuals in deeper and more meaningful ways? Can you find more spiritual connections and create or find sacred places?

If your job requires little emotional effort, bring your heart into your work. Find ways to make the job more personal. If you feel the work is above or below you, aim for contentment in a work environment that is overly challenging or unrewarding. Treat the work as meaningful, valuable, and important, but not to an extreme. People can tell the difference between fake and genuine emotions. Most patrons value competent service and quality products, not emotional presentations, although there are times and professions in which people seek to be uplifted.

It can be easy to put too much emphasis and joy in work. "Guard your heart," as the wise man once said. However, if you place no value and have no heart connection to your work, there is an issue here too.

Evaluate where you are on this spectrum. Are you getting meaning from work or giving meaning to work? It should be the latter, but all too often it is not. If your work gives you meaning, step back emotionally from the work. Certain professions are easier to get caught up in emotionally, such as health care, management, counseling, consulting, service work, and work involving children or vulnerable populations. Work that involves close connections with helping other people can create unhealthy, dependent bonds. If your meaning comes from other people, organizations, or government, then you are no longer in control of your emotions.

Work should allow you to become a better version of yourself. Therefore, your job needs to be treated in a way that allows you to grow. Maybe it only pays the bills, and this is fine. Do not take meaning from it. Give the job meaning.

Assuming your job pays the bills, bring your best self—body, heart, mind, and spirit—into work, but leave room for your growth. Most jobs do more than pay the bills. If a job leaves nothing for personal development, that is an issue in most cases (soldiers and missionaries are exceptions, but those are serious callings).

The last part of bringing your heart into the community is seeking ways to make your community reflect yourself. Can you do the work in a way that is unique to who you are? It's a hard question, but the answer is meaningful. These questions get addressed by the masters— Michelangelo, Beethoven, Jordan, Ford, Gates, and others. They put something of their spirit into their work.

If your job has no spiritual component, bring the spirit into your work. A spiritual application is often easier when preceded by physical, mental, and emotional application. Those disconnected from the spiritual do not instinctively know how to work with spirit. You know exercise, learning, and controlled emotions are good, but you may not instinctively know what to do with your spirit.

Begin learning this by recognizing you are a spiritual being who is also physical, mental, and emotional. You can discipline, focus on, and serve a purpose spiritually, just as your body, mind, and heart can.

How do you unconsciously sabotage your own work? How can you add your full self to what you do? Who are you as a spirit, your intrinsic and unconscious nature? Not to belabor the point, but there are serious religious connotations here. In your work, you can search for spiritual and hidden desires. Seek others to point out where you self-sabotage and study the spiritually enlightened for guidance.

People who integrate spirit into their work can change the world. Consider Martin Luther, George Washington, William Wilberforce, and others. How did they infuse their spirits into their work?

Others typically create your work—a company, product, customers, clients, or out-of-environmental needs. When you integrate meaning into your work, things change. People may not understand or accept what you are doing mentally, as the spirit can seem counterintuitive. It does not seem that most people consider the transient nature of their physical lives on this planet. People fear death—the unknown, the eternal nature of spirit. They may fear changes or be physically unable to cope with a new way. As you connect to spirit and view the world through a metaphysical lens as a uniquely conscious being tied to a deeper eternal reality, the influence and energy of your work will be unique and disruptive.

Little is known here. Many have gone before us in almost every field of work and endeavor. It is a powerfully dangerous endeavor to change the nature of the world. Not that disruption is unimportant; it is indeed important. Progress is vital, but it always ventures into chaos and the unknown. If you do not have your own self and relationships in order, this multiplies the danger of the endeavor by whatever factor your life is not in order. And remember: no life is completely in order.

Be brave, go slow, think and plan, change small things, track and analyze results, and repeat. There are many excellent methods of planning discussed in part II; however, when you mess with systems of the world, careful planning becomes more important. The ripple effects (second order) of change are hard, if not impossible, to measure. You need courage, focus, discipline, and purpose when changing your community.

Growth

If you are making a meaningful, positive difference in your work, while the disruption and unknown remain manageable, you are growing! Sometimes frustration and mistakes do not feel like growth, but errors are substantially how you learn. How do you expand your growth or more deeply influence your community? Grow or expand your influence in your department, company, and beyond.

Confront others' suffering through service, as discussed in chapter 3. How? Serve others' bodies, minds, hearts, and spirits. Identify their needs—where things are difficult and others struggle where you once trod—and offer answers, guidance, and a listening ear. Find a pain point and offer a solution! This is business 101. However, it is difficult to be purposeful with your own life. It's a degree more difficult serving those with whom you have a relationship. And it's an order of magnitude more difficult to serve an entire community.

As you grow, serving others becomes possible because you understand the needs that apply to large groups of people. You understand pain and how to avoid it. So, you tread lightly. It is easy to influence (sell) your communities on pain avoidance techniques. There are three such traps to avoid.

First, if you take responsibility for another's suffering, that person can lose the benefit that suffering inherently offers. This needs careful consideration factoring in people's choices. The best safety nets are healthy individuals and small, localized organizations (even private businesses) that are equipped to deal with individual complexities at the local level. Large, impersonal conglomerations managed by bureaucratic groups cannot do this. The results are always tragic! When you take away suffering caused by error, it decreases the brain's plasticity. You make it harder for people to learn.

Big business and government often think the solution to suffering is more money. It is not. It is more personal responsibility. Reward healthy choices, strong families, and spiritual discipline. Put the responsibility on individuals to know the results of their choices. Never hide results behind corporate tax breaks, complex regulations, or intricate bureaucracies.

Second, if you are in an organization and you take another's suffering, your organization may suffer. If a wealthier country gives money to a poorer country, the taxes of the wealthier country fund this. The wealthier country's population must suffer, but does 100 percent of the wealthier country's population have its house in order? Impossible. Therefore, you must take into consideration how reducing others' suffering will impact those reducing the suffering.

For sure, it is correct to undergo hard, tedious research into curing cancer, understanding the mind and relationships, and designing ways for people to get stronger, healthier, smarter, more emotionally balanced, and more spiritually disciplined. But, have your house in order too. Understand that as communities take on the suffering of others, the community's suffering increases, and not in ways that are proportional to those who can bear it best! Beware unintended consequences.

Third, there is a problem with motive. Why are you taking another's suffering? Is it to suffer for them? There is nothing greater than to lay down your life for another. However, you often help a neighbor not out of the purity of your character, but for recognition or to reduce your future suffering (scratch their back today, and they may scratch yours tomorrow). What is your motive for solving others' pain? It often has to do with power.

Be careful about robbing others of suffering's benefit, consider unanticipated consequences of placing one group's burdens on the shoulders of another, and question the motives of a community/organization/group taking others' suffering. Even with these challenges, you can take the suffering of others and make the world a better place.

Currency, companies, and governments exist because they offer value and ease the exchange of one thing for another. A company can invent a cure for cancer and make the world a better place. Companies can charge for a service that reduces suffering, perhaps by increasing convenience so people can deal with more meaningful suffering and reinvest these returns into improving the world. The government can bear the burden of first-responder services, protecting citizens from disaster, and representing smaller communities on larger stages.

Never trust someone who says, "It's free." If it is valuable, it has a cost. The politician who promises free health care, education, and jobs wants to make people slaves—because nothing is, nor should anything be, free.

Free is the antithesis of *being*. The existence of being has cost. There is always some exchange of matter, relationship, or thought.

A child does not grow alone; the mother sacrifices. Life consumes fuel to grow; one form of life ceases for another to develop. Only in this challenge—the decay of one form for another—can the tree of life take root, sprout, and find meaning and purpose.

To confront suffering, operate in secret. There may come a time when you find the cure for cancer and it is impossible to take this benefit into the world secretly—but avoid the limelight. Do the good, speak the good, share the good, sell the good, and then move on. The best coaches and leaders often operate behind the scenes. History remembers some, but many who are forgotten are equally important. Legacy is more than self; it needs to be self plus something else.

You have yourself—body, heart, mind, and spirit- your relationships, and your work in order. Is there additional work you could do? A way to add value or help the boss? Ease the workload on others? Volunteer? Serve the community? These are good starting points, especially if it is not taking another person's work. You may do it in a way that does not completely change the community, perhaps for a time you do it in secret during your free time. Let those good things come out in a way that others get credit for them. Taking ownership of success is risky, as it can create resentment and mistrust. Let others take the credit.

This is not an excuse to avoid helping others. Just be cognizant of your motives. There is a benefit to helping a neighbor, and it is acceptable to help others, receive the benefit, and live a healthy, happy life. Just do not develop a puffed-up attitude because you did an act of kindness. Your act does not mean you are special. It means you are a halfway decent human being. If you donate a million dollars to the local charity, this is another matter. Always do it in secret or in a way that helps you avoid personal credit.

You can be a being with health, intelligence, and emotional stability who lives in harmony with the divine. Much growth in that direction comes via suffering. In doing what is difficult, challenging yourself, and facing your fears, you can find meaning! It is possible to become a better person!

PART II
SKILL

Chapter 5

INDIVIDUAL SKILLS

The separation of talent and skill is one of the greatest misunderstood concepts for people who are trying to excel, who have dreams, who want to do things. Talent you have naturally. Skill is developed only by hours and hours and hours of beating on your craft.

—Will Smith

A winner is someone who recognizes his God-given talents, works his tail off to develop them into skills, and uses these skills to accomplish his goals.

—Larry Bird

Talents vs. Skill

You are unique. Maybe you are good at sports, have a knack for foreign language, are decent at being a friend, and realize a weakness or two in your spirit. Are these skills or talents? It depends.

People think they are skilled at something when it is easy, and this could be true; however, often the ease with which a person does something shows not skill but talent, a gift.

True skill is found in the balance between ability and inability. The most talented person still has a limit. Skill comes in managing that limit. A skilled racecar driver can maintain the state between a death-causing crash and the upper limits of a vehicle's performance. The driver does this by balancing the physical demands of a high stress-induced heart rate while performing complex mental calculations; communicating with the pit team; controlling fear, anger, or frustration; fighting off self-doubt; and maintaining inner peace. This is skill—but is it ever easy? The driver may have natural talent, but without working at it, that talent will not be enough to survive, much less win.

Talent—innate individual ability—can contribute to your becoming skilled at something, but does it matter? Not completely. Height is obviously a gift that can help in basketball, but there are short professional basketball players. Hearing is important to music, but Beethoven composed while deaf. Nearly 70 percent of billionaires (according to *Forbes*) did not inherit their wealth. And not all painters had hands!

Talent is a starting place. The kid born to be a sports pro, rock star, or spiritual guru is in trouble. There are no free lunches, and a gift can become a curse. That is why Les Brown says, "The graveyard is the richest place on earth." Many children are fearless in art, music, and the stage. They answer what they want to be without fear—fighter pilot, president, and princess. They have talents for many things. Within a few years of school, this changes.

Fear is learned. You get criticized and learn you are not all you could be. You learn you are not good or good enough. This is painful and true. If you are lucky, someone will notice you have a talent for something. They encourage this talent and you think you have a skill. It comes easy, because you are talented. You get decent grades in school, play on a high school team, or win a talent show. Then you live a life of quiet desperation with undeveloped talents. You never realized your skills are not skills. They're talents! You must put in extra time, practice, thought, emotion, and spirit to develop talent into skill.

Everyone has talent. Few develop talent into skill, because it takes hard work, long hours, discipline, and focus. Many go to the grave talented at math without solving the world's great math problems. Many talented football players never go pro. Amazing singers die not having graced the stage—all because of fear of failure or fear of success.

Why fear success? Failure sends you back into obscurity; nobody knows you and everything negative people said about you is proven true. This is unpleasant, but it is not unbearably painful. It is simply returning you to the status quo.

Fear of success is the genuine fear. If success comes via luck and chance, your success will reveal you as a fraud. Yet it goes deeper than this. You must confront the lie of chance. You could have been born in ancient times without all the modern world offers—this is chance. You could have been born poor, a member of a minority group, female, handicapped, suffering from disease, waiting too long to start, having a poor upbringing, having low intelligence, a victim of bad genetics, or whatever other unlucky roll of the dice you can imagine.

Everyone has an excuse. What are you to do—give up, quit, lay down and die, or be the victim? People choose these options all the time. Few choose the other option, which is to do something meaningful and risk failing from the greater height of success.

Developing a skill is meaningful if we have a *why*.

He who has a *why* to live for can bear almost any *how*. (Friedrich Nietzsche)

In a free society, there are choices. The poor can seek ways to better their situation. The minority can rise above discrimination. Look at slaves, POWs, and the horribly oppressed—greats like Frederick Douglass,

Ernest Gordon, and Elie Wiesel. Humans can be oppressed only so far. Humankind can totally oppress physically, partially emotionally and mentally, but never spiritually.

Some choices you make cause pain. Choosing to jump out of an airplane without a parachute is deadly. Being born handicapped presents unique challenges, but what you do with life is largely your choice. If you choose to face your bad luck, it will be hard, but as Frederick Douglass said, "If there is no struggle, there is no progress."

Ernest Gordon wrote about his experience as a prisoner of war in *Through the Valley of the Kwai*. He wrote that the strong and weak, those with and without faith, those who hated, and those who forgave all died. The oppression of death pervaded:

Death was still with us—no doubt about that. But we were being slowly freed from its destructive grip. We were seeing for ourselves the sharp contrasts between the forces that make for life and those that make for death. Selfishness, hatred, jealousy, and greed were all anti-life. Love, self-sacrifice, mercy, and creative faith, on the other hand, were the essence of life, turning mere existence into living in its truest sense.

Doing what it took to survive—not giving up and dying and instead facing their suffering and growing in relationship with God—gave those in Gordon's POW camp purpose. Their misfortune was irrelevant. Doing what is meaningful and purposeful is hard. Success does not make it easy; genuine fear of success is fear of bearing the responsibility of success. It is usually easier to lie down and die.

Love, self-sacrifice, mercy, forgiveness, and faith can be difficult when life is good. Mustering them in the face of tragedy and oppression is even harder. And not to minimize the truly oppressed, but we are all oppressed. If you were born with a silver spoon in your mouth and never earned a thing in life, you suffer the oppression of never knowing struggle. If you are born into royalty, how can you measure up? No matter what other oppressions you face, you are born into time, the greatest oppressor.

Skill is unique to you. Do not play the victim by looking at other people for an excuse. You cannot compare yourself to others, because it offers an unfair choice between victim and victor. Neither encourages personal development. Instead, compare yourself to who you were yesterday. This is the path to developing skill.

Are you living physically, mentally, emotionally, and spiritually better than yesterday? It is a hard question because the ice cream temptation gets you. You zone out too long in front of the TV. You make an emotional decision. You let your spirit become unsettled, your unconscious self takes over, or it gets buried.

Skill is making errors in harmony with yourself. Why harmonize with self? Humans develop skill (a.k.a. learn) by making mistakes—it's how the brain and body work from a scientific standpoint. Without errors, you do not learn! Success does not generate plasticity within your brain to encode knowledge. Errors do. They allow you to recognize the correct way and encode it. Without error, you become a turkey, getting fatter and fatter until November rolls around. By comparing yourself to another person, you do not learn from your errors. Make errors! Otherwise, you are at odds with your becoming.

Every day is a new day, and setbacks are part of life. Start from where you are, and aim for minor improvements. Let the mistakes guide you, increasing your brain's plasticity through emotional discomfort until you reach success. Errors chemically prime your brain for learning.

Marcus Aurelius pointed out, "The mind adapts and converts to its own purposes the obstacle to our acting. The impediment to action advances action. What stands in the way becomes the way."

Skill is a choice. Avoid relying on natural talents that shelter you from mistakes. When your natural talents bring success, you do not learn. And you cannot afford to be unskilled! You must push the limits of your physical, mental, emotional, and spiritual being. Don't push your limits until you make mistakes, and you do not learn. This puts you in a fragile place that allows victimization. Within the constraints of your environment, choose to become less vulnerable.

Skills

In the previous section I discussed skill, the difference between talent and skill, avoiding skill development because of fear, and how facing suffering through error leads toward growth. Now it's time for a deeper dive into skills. You want skill in utilizing your full being to your full potential. However, this does not define at what you want to be skilled.

Start by focusing on your strengths and working to mitigate your weaknesses. All people have individual physical strengths and weaknesses—they're taller, shorter, stockier, leaner, etc. Learning your physical characteristics and developing them takes discipline that results in skill.

In the relational/heart aspect, consider the introvert and the extrovert. Introverts should learn to speak in public to get the job done. The extrovert should develop skill at sitting quietly alone and thinking through a problem. Introverts do not have to become Broadway stars and extroverts do not have to enter actuarial services. You have unique perspectives on relationships and complex emotional strengths and weaknesses. Develop skills that mitigate these weaknesses and complement your strengths.

You should also consider the people and environment around you. The questions "What is the environment?" and "Who are the people?" are important to answer. What do the people surrounding you need? What does the environment around you offer or threaten? The answers help inform the direction your skills should be developed. Understanding your environment helps identify needed skill development. (More on this in parts 3 and 4.)

Think of people as the market needing your skills. This includes your family, employer, coworkers, and community. A family needs love and attention. Employers need particular types of employees. Coworkers need good teammates. Your community has a diverse set of needs. Skills that meet the needs of your "marketplace" of people are good to develop.

Skills are situationally dependent. They're developing, changing, and being individualized based on the individual. Who you are today cannot be the person you will be tomorrow. You cannot afford to be stagnant in life. There are fundamental skills that provide good ways to start your growth. As you learn the basics, spread out and specialize in the following:

- Thinking: Thinking should be the point of all education. Learning how to think is difficult, and school systems should do better, but you cannot allow yourself to be a victim of this failure.
- Reading: Reading and reading comprehension are important. There is a reason educators begin teaching reading in elementary school and never stop. It is important. Think carefully about what you read.
- Writing: Writing is the act of making your thoughts tangible. Writing about reading is tangibly thinking about what you read and helps internalize it. You can write about the past (learn from it), the present (what it means), and the future (where you want to go). In this way you can understand yourself, deal with your place in the present, and develop plans to seek meaning.
- Living: This can depend on environment, but how can you live physically? This includes eating healthily, understanding your sleep needs and patterns (circadian rhythm), getting adequate exercise, and setting your life in order to have stability from which you experiment and venture out into the world's chaos.
- Job: Be skilled at what you do! This affords the opportunity to build a stable life and pay the bills.
- Relationships: Though unique, people have similarities and consistencies. Understanding and dealing with relationships helps you navigate a world in which relationships are critical.
- Theology: What is your relationship to the spiritual? This is the most important subject because it answers a lot about your psychology and has implications on the weight and direction you place on meaning and purpose in life. It is a constantly developing skill, and you will go through seasons as your relationship to the divine changes.

From here, you have a good foundation on which to build. A few other skills are also important for their ability to make you less fragile: business/commerce, self-defense, basic finance, politics/diplomacy, and artistic endeavors to name a few.

Business/commerce extends job skills and wields the ability to create your own job, providing freedom from an employer. Self-defense grants you the ability to live in the world without fear of an individual's power over you, which leads to a healthier mindset. Finance skills allow you to build mathematical engines for generating wealth for self, family, and community. Politics/diplomacy extends into relationships and lets you navigate personal relationships at a deeper level as well as perceive larger political machinations. Finally, there are skills that make you more complete through self-expression in artistic endeavors.

Face the risk of making mistakes. If you know you are going to make mistakes, start small and practice. A child learns to read with the smallest pieces of language and practices it over and over. Granted, children's brains are substantially different from those of adults over age twenty-six. Children's learning pathways (brain plasticity) are completely open. Children can soak up information, language, and facts, and their errors usually enforce limits and reduce mental pathways. Therefore, handle children with care and compassion!

After age twenty-six, you do not learn the same. For adults to change their brains, they must make errors to open brain plasticity to help the brain recognize success. Without error for comparison, the neurological settings will not embed the correct learning. Therefore, when learning, start small. You can learn from catastrophe (if you survive), but it is not recommended or sustainable.

How to learn:

- Thinking: Start small and simple. Get a journal. Take two minutes to sit and think, then two minutes to write your thoughts. This should be a scheduled, intentional activity. What keeps you from thinking? What distractions/errors disrupt your taking time to think?

- Planning: Plans needs to be tangible. Planning in a meaningful and actionable way allows you to execute the plan—no small feat and a powerful skill. Plans provide concrete evidence of errors and successes. They help to lean into the errors for growth. Grab a calendar and start planning.

- Time Management: Time is your most valuable resource and comes in a limited, unknown quantity. Using your time in the most effective way can yield results (effectiveness over efficiency). You need time to practice those skills, more time making errors! Where do you make errors in using your time? Why do you always feel so busy?
- Reading: Jot notes about what you read. Grow the habit of studying skill development. Apply thinking about reading—where are you wrong, where are you right, what can you apply and use to avoid making the same error repeatedly?
- Writing: Make notes; analyze your past, present, and future. What lessons did you learn in the past? Are they helpful or harmful? What are you learning today? What do you think the present is teaching you? When you look back on your past writing, were you correct or in error? How did your plans turn out?
- Living: Clean your house, fix your porch, work on your landscaping, get life in order, and figure out where you fall short.
- Job: Think about, study, and analyze your job. Practice doing it better, faster, and cheaper, and then ask for more and more.
- Relationships: Talk to people, including strangers; make a friend; be a friend or ask friends how you could be a better friend. Seek criticism regarding what you lack and then practice improving. If you have a family, they know where you are lacking; find out, improve, and repeat.
- Theology: Visit a religious community; ask for guidance from religious leaders. As stated previously, the most important question is not how—but why. If you want to compare yourself to someone, compare yourself to who you could be from a religious perspective!

The Way

If you know the way broadly, you will see it in everything. (Miyamoto Musashi)

Learning a skill applies across the range of other skills. Japanese samurai knew this centuries ago. Their sword skills flowed into art, calligraphy, leadership, and government.

At first, it is difficult to learn, but eventually your ability can take off. At the inflection point of critical mass, you will get scared. This makes sense, because learning skills is a step into the unknown. You do not know what it will take to learn it. You may fall, receive criticism, become lost, or suffer other pains when traveling out of your comfort zone. Unfortunately, you may have learned that failure is not okay. It is. Let go of the failure, get back up, and try again.

Sometimes, you work hard to learn something, only to scurry to stop that ball from rolling ahead. You realize you want to stay where you are, where life is safe and familiar. This is logical. You want to consolidate your wins (cover your bases). However, this can be dangerous because of the rules of momentum. A body in motion wants to stay in motion; a body at rest takes more energy to start.

Harness your growth. Take the new job assignment, push your body when tired, read a book that is difficult to comprehend, put your emotions into something meaningful, and confront your subconscious fears. Doing this helps you develop as a being. As you do, the cost of mistakes will grow, your suffering will increase, and your life will take on more meaning.

You can quantify this from a business perspective. A sole proprietorship failing may affect one person, whereas a multinational corporation affects thousands. You cannot deal with the failure of the latter without first learning to deal with the failure of the first.

Enjoyably, you can branch out. The better you become at living, thinking, feeling, and being, the deeper and broader you can go into these aspects. The deeper and broader you go, the deeper and broader you are able to ease suffering. The great samurai Miyamoto Musashi set out to learn the art of war and drank so deeply from it that he found peace and enlightenment. Think and learn as deeply and broadly as you can.

Chapter 6

RELATIONSHIP SKILLS

God created humankind in his image, in the image of God he created them; male and female he created them. God blessed them and God said to them, "Be fruitful and multiply, and fill the land, and conquer it."

—Genesis 1:27–28 NRSV

Any man's death diminishes me, because I am involved in mankind, and therefore never send to know for whom the bell tolls. It tolls for thee.

—John Donne

Relational Aspects of Skill

Relationship skills are important skills. "No man is an island," wrote John Donne.

All the great religious writings are about relationship. Primary is your relationship with the divine. Additionally, God made people to have relationships, the highest of which is matrimony, a model of the perfect relationship. Relationships establish order amidst chaos. You see this in religious writings and natural law when love produces children and thus another model of relationship, that of parent to child. The sages, independent of religious affiliation, repeat the importance of relationships:

Nature bore us related to one another. Like an arch of stones, which would fall apart if they did not support each other. (Seneca)

This expands to student, teacher, and partner relationships, discussed in chapter 3.

The student aspect of relationships makes common sense. You develop skill by being a student. Treat your world and others as your teacher, and you will learn more skill. It is important to find outstanding teachers. It is equally important to learn from all others and the world.

One of the best ways to further your own skills is to teach them to others. This forces you to express your skills in a way others can comprehend and learn for themselves. Like learning, teaching is a skill.

Finally, being a fit partner is a skill. Good partnerships are powerful because the whole is more than the sum of the parts. Partners who work well together always deliver greater results than they can separately. Adam Smith's *Wealth of Nations* detailed this by describing the "specialization of labor." However, this doesn't apply only on a grand scale of nations and corporations but also at an individual level. The specialization of labor was a revolutionary idea for large-scale economies, but it is also important for partnerships at an individual level.

The key to better relationships is bringing each partner's uniqueness and individuality into the present as a student, teacher, and partner without holding on to the past or worrying about the future. This takes honesty, openness, and awareness of strengths and weaknesses.

The Student Skill

You are reading this book, which implies you were once a reading student. Learning skills takes hard work and a recognition of your need to learn. Sadly, the coddling of children educationally is worsening. The West is now in a long-term downward educational trend. This creates confusion about the power and importance of being a student.

One of the greatest things you can learn is that you are ignorant. The recognition of your knowledge limits and capacity is huge. To become an outstanding student takes humility. "Empty your cup so that it may be filled," said Bruce Lee. Better still, Jesus said, "Come to me as a little child."

When entering adulthood, three things affect your need for humility. Your ability to identify patterns declines (Basu 2021); your prefrontal cortex finishes developing, increasing control over executive decision-making; and your brain becomes hardened to change (Cummins 2021). These changes decrease the plasticity of your brain. Without such changes, you would be left to the tedious task of constantly relearning the hard lessons of youth. Though such changes are a blessing, they make it harder to be a student. Brain plasticity (neuroplasticity) refers to neurons—the building blocks of the brain— and the brain's ability to change. The adult prefrontal cortex takes a larger role in learning and provides increased error detection, specifically when errors are more costly, performance is being evaluated, and there is increased anxiety (Hajcak 2021). This appears beneficial for survival, for adult errors would feel more costly.

Evolutionarily, you learn, execute on your knowledge, perpetuate the species, and die. But modern humans want more. Errors are critical. They cause the brain's synapses to kick in and investigate unknown patterns. You then must focus on the error-induced pain to increase adrenaline and open your brain to recognizing the correct pattern. You must "lean into the errors" (Huberman 2021).

A mind that thinks it knows something will struggle to grow. It will avoid uncomfortable errors and disregard minor errors. A conceited mind will not struggle. It will remain ignorant.

You may feel smart, but humans do not know the answers to many of the following:

- When, where, and what was the first domesticated dog?
- What is the physics of foam?
- What are colors?
- What is time?
- What happened to the Neanderthal?
- How do entangled particles communicate?
- How does a brain produce consciousness?

Not that you know nothing. There are things you can know for a time or for yourself. You can identify actions that create reactions and a few other laws until you reach the outer edges of our scales where laws do not apply. As Jesus and Bruce Lee taught, you must let go of your assumptions, humble yourself, and open your mind to what little pieces of information and knowledge are available.

As a youth, you strive to carve a place for yourself because you lack a fully developed prefrontal cortex. The danger is thinking this place-carving stops.

Just because you gain executive-level decision-making skill, does not mean you should quit learning. This lesson gets repeated throughout history. Adam and Eve assumed they knew better than God; eleven sons of Jacob thought they knew better than Joseph; people said Socrates was the wisest in Athens because he realized his ignorance; and Andrew Grove, CEO of Intel, wrote in *Only the Paranoid Survive*:

Admitting that you need to learn something new is always difficult. It is even harder if you are a senior manager who is accustomed to the automatic deference which people accord you owing to your position. But if you don't fight it, that very deference may become a wall that isolates you from learning new things. It all takes self-discipline.

Self-discipline and humility can be a challenge to develop, particularly as you move further into success. The trappings of success are many and degrade discipline and humility. Religion offers antidotes to ego. Faced with an all-knowing God, enlightenment, and other transcendent ideas, your own intelligence seems less significant. "Pride comes before destruction" is played out through history in the deaths of hundreds of millions via holocausts, gulags, and great leaps forward. These egotistical ideologies wear new masks today and are reemerging with new vehemence.

Start the day humbly by learning something, getting the ego crushed, challenging and struggling. Then be mindful of this all day long. You cannot fake it; ego always has a price. The longer you hold onto ego, the further the fall!

The humble find outstanding teachers who teach on physical, mental, emotional, and spiritual matters. Take their knowledge and apply it throughout life. Remember, teachers are not an elite group with a set role. A teacher is any person with knowledge you lack.

Doctors are a resource to diagnose and treat illness. Most also know a substantial amount about exercise and nutrition. These are the best medicines. They decrease sickness and increase energy, endurance, and longevity. If your doctor appears physically fit (a good sign), ask what your physician does to maintain their health. Then do likewise.

Schools are filled with teachers who have book knowledge, which is where much knowledge starts. Just keep in mind that what works in a classroom rarely works in the field. The real world brings errors and allows for learning and growth. Professional mentorship is invaluable in this regard.

It is a rare teacher who teaches how to be self-sufficient and benefit society. Learning your job or career means you can earn a paycheck and add to the system instead of taking from it. A teacher who teaches good work ethic is invaluable. Mentorship is important for body, mind, heart, and spirit, but you will outgrow mentors and need to move on. Do not give in to the comfortable place under the tutelage of a familiar teacher and thus stagnate.

In the modern age, your mental teachers should be broad—this is the

Information Age, after all. In a free society, you have choices regarding how to plan, invest, and save for the future. Criticisms of capitalism, financial exchange, and free markets that create haves and have-nots revolve around free will. These systems are about freedom and free will, and critiques of these systems create minimal answers outside of reducing freedom. Investing wisely can lead to a better future for all, including yourself. There is good and bad advice on this subject. Look at the individuals who are earning by investing and teaching as a way to give back. More on finances is in part V and chapter 14.

Relationship coaches often double as spiritual coaches. Some of the best relationship advice is spiritual advice translated to fit relationships. If you believe any of the great religions, the fundamental first belief is that God made us for a relationship with himself and each other.

Philosopher Nassim Taleb says, "Love without sacrifice is like theft." A good relationship requires that you give. To paraphrase Emerson, "To have a friend, be a friend." For good relationships, do something and give something, without seeking something in return. A relationship teacher teaches you how to listen better, give your time better, give your resources better, and more. They require the individual seeking relationship advice to change!

Accepting yourself as you are is terrible advice. You are not as self-aware as you think. Because of this, you receive the best advice from those closest to you. Your parents, spouse, children, boss, neighbor, coworkers, and friends often know what you are doing wrong. But fear of confrontation causes them to shy from saying anything critical. It is a giant ego-killer to ask for criticism, but it's essential. Just do it the right way. Do not ask without being willing to act, as not acting can make things worse.

Spiritual teachers have tasks similar to relationship teachers, as your true self is harder to see. Others can often recognize your traits better than you can. The same is true of spiritual teachers.

Your spiritual self is your connection to the divine and eternal (see chapter 2). It drives your mind, fights your flesh and emotions, and gives you the gift of story. Spiritual knowledge and wisdom are rare. Your father and mother are your first spiritual teachers. The great stories teach that when you embark on the journey of growth and enlightenment, you will find and/or rediscover your parents. The cultural destruction of families and the failings of weak parents who reject hard-won traditions endanger future generations in ways unfathomable.

Wealth and excess cloud the First World with the material and eclipse the spiritual. The world is entering dangerous territory when parents do not teach spiritual and emotional wisdom, disregarding a thousand years of history. An ancient Greek saying claims that separating scholars from warriors results in laws made by cowards and wars fought by fools. When we pass on a compartmentalized perspective of what it means to be human, we rob future generations of part of humanity's richness.

This leads me to an important point. You can be a student of those who came before us. This is required when you cannot find the wise among you. Wisdom is best seen through time. Learning from those who came before allows you to increase the learning cycle. If you discard the past and dialectically tear down systems, meaningful foundation is lost.

Civilization's systems preserve and allow access to wisdom. Take advantage of this. Those who speak out of history can be your teachers if you humble yourself before their wisdom. The ancient Israelites, Greeks, Romans, and others teach important things. Look at the history of their ideas. Their wisdom has survived because of merit.

Likewise, you can learn from failed, deteriorating ideologies that have resulted in suffering. But be warned: failed ideologies constantly change from Marxism to postmodernism to Chinese communism to democratic socialism. The depth of knowledge readily available to you from the ancient and classical past contains lifetimes of lessons.

You can also learn from others who are learning from the wisdom of the ages. Books, the internet, video streaming services, and podcasts allow you to learn efficiently from those who have learned lessons already. New media has increased the distribution of information and wisdom. A fun example is martial arts. Before modern media, sleight of hand, mentalism, and other psychological tricks made people believe that certain martial arts were more effective. The internet is filled with videos debunking "fake" martial arts promoting nerve strikes, no-touch knockouts, and other silliness.

In the final year of writing this book, there has been an increase in corporate censorship of alternative media that may have a downward impact on new media's ability to increase knowledge. Censorship that reduces new media's ability to call out groups like Chinese autocratic leadership, promote effective health care that reduces reliance on pharmaceuticals, silences political opponents, encourages society's movement toward oppression, and overtly uses media to manipulate elections is dangerous.

The abundance of new media means you must be careful of confirmation bias. You want to believe what is easy, spectacular, or fits your preconceived notions of the world. Thankfully, as the world grows more interconnected, what does not work in nutrition, exercise, finance, work, relationships, and other areas is being exposed. Hopefully, this continues.

Remember, what sounds good is not always good. What sounds hard, difficult, and achieved with effort, consistency, and discipline is more likely to be legitimate and worth the effort. The test is whether something really works. More and more, these tests are conducted and documented for you, but you can run tests, too. If guidance does not lead to the right result, switch. Right effort is the bigger challenge. What worked a thousand years ago is more likely to work than what worked a hundred years ago. And what worked a hundred years ago is more likely to work than what is new.

The last key to being an outstanding student is internalizing information so that you apply it. Knowledge without application is a waste. When young, you do not know what knowledge will be valuable for your life. You are just trying to survive and struggle with prefrontal cortex development. As you age, seek knowledge for the sake of knowledge; later, for usefulness.

If wise, you will learn what to do and not to do from your environment. Where your parents were virtuous and good, follow. Where their lives bore poor fruit, stay away. As you become older and your knowledge spreads and becomes more specialized, seeking knowledge for knowledge's sake becomes a challenge. Such seeking can be driven by ego and pride. Ego and pride then lead to confirmation bias, which leads to actions that cause suffering and harm.

In summary, the key to being an excellent student is humility before that which works—emotionally engaged and focused learning—followed by internalizing it for life application.

Teacher

Being a teacher runs significant risk. A teacher who teaches what does not work or what is untrue misleads. Intentional misleading is despicable. There is nothing worse than an abusive religious leader, a dishonest elected official, a thieving financial adviser, or a pill-pushing health care provider. Each lead away from proper character, betraying themselves and those they teach. It's the worst of all sins, and the famous poet Dante reserved the worst circle of hell for betrayers.

Misleading knowingly is the height of evil, but misleading unknowingly also leads toward destruction. It is the consequence of pride, what happens when you fail to inspect and confirm unbiasedly. Typically, you assume you know something when it sounds good, feels good, seems good, and will probably make others feel good. Causing others to feel good can increase pride. Unfortunately, pride is a path leading toward incomplete investigation and jumping to conclusions. This is unfortunate when the prideful individual suffers the consequences. It is tragic when such a faulty worldview is taught to others.

Though no teacher or person is perfect, take responsibility for anything you teach. To be an excellent teacher, speak the truth. This requires discernment, what the ancient philosophers called *logic* or the *discipline of assent*. Like students, teachers require humility to discern what is true, false, and unknown. No teacher holds all truth and untruth; you must therefore remain humble and admit you don't know certain things. This is challenging for teachers who are expected and even paid to know.

Before speaking the truth, you must know the truth. Through

the ages, great minds have argued several hypotheses regarding truth: that there is none, it is unknowable, it is malleable and only partially knowable, and it is absolute.

Dispense with the first two. If there is no truth or the truth is unknowable, put this book down and go read gibberish. The first two are possible only for the deluded, delusional, or truly evil. Such ideas are logically self-defeating. How can you know anything if there is nothing to know? If truth is unknowable, you cannot know truth to be unknowable; therefore, it is self-eliminating. The only two options are that truth is changing and partially reliable, or that truth is absolute.

Absolute cannot be proven in a physical and empirical world because of the limitations of such a world. You are bound by time and space. You cannot know or test a hypothesis over the ages. You were not present at the beginning of the universe, nor will you be present at its end. Still, the reality of time and space point to truth. Many physical and logical things may not apply to emotional or spiritual things. The divine may reveal parts of absolute truth, which requires individual interpretation as the individual expresses this through their own understanding within time and space.

For this book (there are entire tomes about truth), truth as partially known and subject to the individual person, situation, and circumstances indicates your orientation in space and time. The absolute truth from the divine's perspective is important and knowable, but beyond the scope of this book.

You need to discern truth at a given place and time. Truth (meaning) is found in life. The challenge is knowing what is meaningful from your time and space orientation. You may look at this is from a utilitarian position (what works is true), but this view is incomplete as it focuses only on ends. Radiation may clean a bathroom, but it kills the owner; bleach takes more work, but is a better choice.

You must focus on the means. This happens when you act with love and humility toward the world, its systems, and its people. It is where meaning confronts suffering and causes your growth. Who you are, where you find yourself, and what you orient toward matter. Your relationship toward others, position in the environment, and resources are expanded on in parts III, IV, and V of this book.

If you are a student of the truth, then you will constantly reorient yourself to the truth. The best teachers are students first. As you learn, apply, adopt, and adapt, you will adjust as you figure out what gives more meaning. A history teacher who uncovers new ways of orienting toward the truth will teach history in a more meaningful way. A gym instructor learns and shares new ways of targeting muscles, fat loss, cardiovascular health, and cleaner living. Some truths are more rigid, others more malleable. Acceptable dress in Florida differs greatly from acceptable dress in Alaska. Truth on a small scale seldom works at a large scale.

It is easier (although difficult) to recognize and orient to the truth in small, simple things. Your body, mind, and heart are good places to start, but as a teacher, you must expand beyond yourself. The problems explode in complex and unique ways when you expand into the meaning of physical, mental, emotional, and spiritual things. This requires judgment and discernment.

It is easy to avoid difficult things, to look only at facts and ignore meaning. But significance matters more than the material facts. When you fail to embark into the unknown and confront the world of chaos, suffering will grow!

Jewish History: In Genesis 12, Abram is told to embark into the unknown and he will be blessed.

"Go from your country, your people and your father's household to the land I will show you." (Genesis 12:1 NIV)

Greek History: Socrates tells Greeks that suffering is a part of life, fundamental to our nature.

If you don't get what you want, you suffer; if you get what you don't want, you suffer; even when you get exactly what you want, you still suffer because you can't hold on to it forever. Your mind is your predicament. It wants to be free of change. Free of pain, free of the obligations of life and death. But change is law and no amount of pretending will alter that reality.

Christian History: In Luke 9, Jesus tells all to confront suffering.

Then He said to them all, "If anyone desires to come after Me, let him deny himself, and take up his cross daily, and follow Me." (Luke 9:23 NKJV)

Roman History: Marcus Aurelius understood pride and ego must die in order to face the world and live in the moment.

Ask: What is so unbearable about this situation? Why can't you endure it? You will be embarrassed to answer.

Eastern History: Let go of much and turn toward suffering. This process lessens suffering on the whole but can increase it on the individual.

The root of suffering is attachment.

European History:

Never shall I forget that night, the first night in camp, which has turned my life into one long night, seven times cursed and seven times sealed. . . . Never shall I forget those moments which murdered my God and my soul and turned my dreams to dust. Never shall I forget these things, even if I am condemned to live as long as God Himself. Never.

Elie Wiesel in his book *Night* exposes the cost of failing to turn toward suffering, allowing ordinary men to do horrible things.

I have nothing to offer but blood, toil, tears and sweat. We have before us an ordeal of the most grievous kind. We have before us many, many long months of struggle and of suffering. (Winston Churchill)

People waited too long to confront suffering. Because of this, those like Wiesel suffered tremendously and those who now had to face suffering or annihilation would suffer greater.

Bless you prison, bless you for being in my life. For there, lying upon the rotting prison straw, I came to realize that the object of life is not prosperity as we are made to believe, but the maturity of the human soul. (Alexander Solzhenitsyn)

Solzhenitsyn understood the truth Russian gulags reveal. The truth, the easy path, is the lie. Evil is always around the corner in your own heart. What you teach should bend toward the truth of being!

Yes, these lessons judge individuals, relationships, and communities. They call out the coward, the weak, the ignorant, the immature, the emotional, and the spiritless. History is a teacher and an example. However, this lesson goes beyond history. It applies to physical things— diet and exercise; mental things—science and math; emotional things— psychology and art; and spiritual things—religion and meaning. Get your house in order so you can help others when the chaos reaches their doorstep.

History is mid-tier in complexity. Physical fitness is relatively simple. It is under a single individual's control, something that most can get here and now, and something you know a fair amount about. Yet many people refuse to do anything about it as global obesity rates skyrocket. Fad diets, diet pills, workout equipment, medical industry, and other businesses make untold fortunes on people's refusal to choose the right path.

Sometimes the solution is simple, not complex. Is it hard? Yes. Will it be uncomfortable? Yes. But most can learn to be fit. Despite this, more will buy a pill or drink a fad shake. Even more will say that they do not have the time or their problem is genetic. America would experience a revolution if government schools made fitness a component of primary education as it was in the 1950s and 1960s.

If teaching the truth about something as simple as physical fitness is so hard, what about everything else? If teachers properly oriented themselves, the revolution would be unstoppable. Unfortunately, government schools prefer the destructive path, allowing easy money to ruin universities and businesses. The path of least resistance is, unfortunately, the more common path. Those in the government school systems taking the hard path are doing the work of saints.

Knowing the truth is a matter of orientation. You confront challenges in your life and are growing as a result, becoming more, but why are you becoming more? As you approach absolute truth, the answers dawn. The best truth fully answers the question *Why?*

The truth can be fact. Scientific truth is truth (until the science changes), but only in a narrow and tightly defined way. Higher truth gives useful meaning. Typically, reaching higher truth is not an easy process. Like the rest of mankind, you are caught up in the material, and the transcendent seems mysterious and strange.

Truth is subject to your orientation within an environment and the resources available for use. However, orientation toward meaning matters. Ultimately, orientation toward God provides humility and the speaking of greater truth. You cannot face God fully without being humbled. Being crucified with Christ is the highest truth I know. Answers to *why* reside in the Word of the great creator God, I Am.

Partnership

Adam Smith's *Wealth of Nations* discusses the "specialization of labor." This says that in a company, an individual should specialize and become good at one thing. Specialization allows cooperation and teamwork to be more effective and efficient. Partnerships built around unique values and differences of individuals yield better results than those built around similarities. There is substantial danger here of confirmation bias. If all partners agree, there is potential that no one is learning, growing, or being challenged. To be an excellent partner, know yourself, be humble, and put the other first.

Knowing yourself is not always easy. To do so, you must place yourself in challenging positions and circumstances. Your ego wants to say that you can handle such challenges, but until you do, you are unsure. How do you handle rejection, failure, loss, poverty, pain, sickness, loneliness, and life challenges that reveal more of yourself? Self-knowledge comes at a cost (more on this in chapter 8).

The best partnerships involves equals as close as manageable (see chapter 3 on partnerships). Partnerships are not always controllable. To manage inherent inequality, partnerships require humility and self-sacrifice of the stronger, better self-actualized partner.

With different partners, you must encourage, listen, and learn. Know your strengths and skills and work on building, using, and leveraging them. Skilled partners meaningfully advance the cause of the partnership. The most fundamental partnership is marriage. Men and women are undeniably different and should encourage and support each other's differences. Husbands and wives who do not try to usurp roles form strong bonds. Business partnerships that recognize the strengths of each partner and allow both to fully use their unique skills create a powerful organization.

Humility means not placing your strength above others' strengths. Does the physical strength of men make them superior to women? The beauty of an attractive woman dominates men consistently. What you perceive as superior is not always the case. The quiet, gentle, soft, peaceful, and supple contain power and strength. Loudness, force, physical power, aggressiveness, and harshness have value, but these characteristics are defaults that are often overused.

Give in to your partners! Seek compromise. However, since you cannot always know what your partner is thinking, default to the student so you can learn. Never default to teacher. If you do not believe your partner's decision is the best, carefully express this. Then help your partner succeed; and if your partner fails with your help, admire and respect your partner for risking the endeavor. Such an approach confirms to your partner that it is fine to make mistakes in your presence. It shows that you support them even when you disagree and that you are learning together.

Nothing makes partnerships stronger than failure. A single touch of a passive-aggressive "I told you so" torches the greatest partnership opportunities.

Humility

Humility runs through any relationship skill. For the student, humility allows the self to be open to growth. For the teacher, it guards against untruth. For partnerships, it allows two individuals to be individuals without seeking dominance.

The most important relationship is that of a student, which defaults toward humility. You graduate from school and think you know it all. Wrong. You have partners, but seek to "bring them up to your level." Wrong. You easily forget the lesson of the student, the importance of humility.

Set it in your mind to be humble. Cultivating humility is at the root of meaningful relationships. You cultivate humility by being quiet, listening with an open mind, seeking to understand, asking questions, and proceeding from the assumption that you know little about anything.

> Do you wish to rise? Begin by descending. You plan a tower that will pierce the clouds? Lay first the foundation of humility. (Augustine)

Chapter 7

LEADERSHIP SKILLS

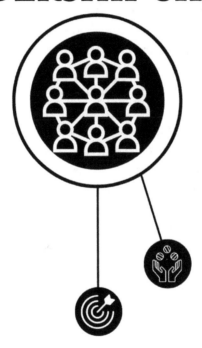

When a country has the skill and self-confidence to take action against its biggest problems, it makes outsiders eager to be a part of it.
—Bill Gates

An incentive is a bullet, a key: an often tiny object with astonishing power to change a situation.

—Steven Levitt

Leadership Challenge

Relationship skills thrive on humility. Community comprises many individual relationships and always has a hierarchical structure. Modernity criticizes hierarchical structure as unhealthy because people feel they create haves and have-nots. Though true to an extent, this does not mean hierarchies are bad or good. It means most people do not understand leadership.

Hierarchies exist in nature. They occur when things naturally organize toward something of value. You recognize this as leadership and, ultimately, God. If all leaders lead with humility, hierarchical structures would improve, but they would still exist.

Not all people live with humility. There are weak, lazy, willfully ignorant, immature, and even spiritless people—usually non-leaders. It is not your place to change them, and seldom your place to judge. That said, do not humble yourself before the weak or give in to the lazy. Be unafraid of strength and discipline. Relish truth, even when people prefer lies. Avoid the immature so you can be content and balanced. Never deny the spirit. As you exist within communities with imperfect people, be an object lesson to others in humility. Point to the ideal community.

Leadership builds communities into hierarchies that reward individuals for who they are. A leader, therefore, focuses on designing and articulating incentives through culture, law, or policy. Each community needs certain skills, depending on the purpose for which the community exists. A software company must be skilled at making software, and a town must be skilled at attracting citizens. A community finds meaning and success to the degree that it rewards meaningful individual skill, humility, truth, and self-sacrifice.

Incentive is central to economics and theorizes how people, partners, organizations, and communities behave given incentivized structure. There are multiple parts to correctly incentivize people to act. The same thing does not engage all people, nor will a community want to reward all its citizens. A town may prefer to incentivize law-abiding citizens, and a software company may prefer to incentivize those with programming skills.

Whatever community you find yourself in, design incentives in line with the resources at your disposal. Do not offer bonuses with cash your business does not have or promote a beach town if you are mayor of a mountain city. Articulate the incentive. Misinterpretation happens with overly complex incentives.

The corollary to incentive is disincentive, but they are not exact opposites. Disincentives are for gaming the incentive—fake skill, false humility, disguising the truth, and sacrificing others. The reason disincentives warn against gaming the system is to allow individuals and relationships to flourish and develop. Disincentives, then, focus on the means more than the ends.

Naturally, reward, respect, and empower the skilled, humble, truth speakers, and self-sacrificers. The problem arises from deceit. For example, the programmer's code that does not work is failure. The programmer should not be punished; he will learn from his mistakes and grow. After all, failure creates growth that leads to success. Fakers, liars, cheats, and thieves must get punished for hiding inability and an unwillingness to learn and grow. The weak, lazy, ignorant, immature, and spiritless pay their own price through natural law if the community encourages people to have skin in the game.

Understand that the weak, lazy, ignorant, immature, and spiritless may not have a choice in the matter. But, it is not easy to decipher what is strong or weak. Is a wheelchair-bound man weaker than a heavyweight boxer? Only the boxer and the man in the wheelchair can answer. What if I said the boxer is Mike Tyson, the youngest undisputed world heavyweight champion of all time and the man in the wheelchair is Stephen Hawking, one of the greatest minds of our time?

A community that judges, rewards, taxes, or pays unequally is dysfunctional. Arrogance and ignorance cause suffering and collapse by focusing on the ends, not the means. A community should encourage all to push the limits of becoming without judging who they consider weak, strong, lazy, hardworking, ignorant, smart, spiritless, or strong spirited. Reward result, punish the liar and cheat, and focus on means.

If you are a community leader, humble yourself. This could mean removing yourself from leadership. If you were set up for failure, it is better to be removed humbly than by a prideful fall. Politicians and leaders acting as the ones who will save us, the planet, or the economy pose a serious problem. This is the opposite of humility. Transformational leadership is not path-making—it is direction-pointing.

Once you humble yourself, get out of the way. Learn to listen and support; let others describe the community's strengths and skills. This will enable leadership to articulate a vision for the community where skill, humility, truth, and self-sacrifice get rewarded.

Next, design a system for incentivizing skill, humility, truth, and self-sacrifice. Then purge the faker, cheater, liar, or spiritless from the community. A church that does not confront sin is dead. A community that allows the violent and criminal to thrive is dead. A business that pays someone not to add value is bankrupt. An organization that rewards and protects the unskilled courts revolution.

The last section of chapter 6 addressed humility. Vision, incentive, and protection need to be addressed in a little more detail.

Vision

Leadership's primary job is articulating a vision of the future. This is complex and cannot be created in a vacuum. Ideally, you discover vision, not create it. Part of what you discover is that the purpose of a community is to serve individuals.

Community purpose should overlap with skills present in the community; the market or people served by the community; the environment, industry, or competitive landscape in which the community finds itself; and the resources available to the community.

Quality leadership seeks to understand the abilities and resources of those within the community. Leadership learns about the people and the environment in which the community operates. In this way, the leader is positioned to articulate a vision based on the real world that strives for something beyond the physical, mental, and emotional. This vision or purpose gives meaning by pushing those involved beyond themselves and into legacy.

Vision articulates where purpose, skill, people, environment, and resources overlap. It is the fig tree of a fruitful life at the center of the five-circle Venn diagram. There are many purposes, skills, types of people, environments, and resources that do not apply to each other.

A skilled pianist without a piano (resource) may not serve others (people) with her piano abilities, particularly if other skilled pianists have access to pianos. What does the pianist do in this situation? If the pianist finds meaning in playing piano for others, the pianist is in danger of becoming a victim of a false ideology. The pianist can become frustrated, suspect a conspiracy, and ultimately become a victim. An alternative meaning (purpose) could be for the pianist to gain the resources of a piano. This changes the skills, people, and environment the pianist must bring to the table. She may need to become a clerk, accountant, or nurse and not solely a pianist.

Many powerful vision statements have been shared across the world, throughout time, in all types of communities. Microsoft founder Bill Gates envisioned "a computer in every home." The Founding Fathers of the United States believed in government in which "power was derived from the people, government existed to benefit the people, and people had undeniable rights." Religious creeds span millennia. The most visionary statements fit within the framework of the five principles.

Note that the Venn diagram's five circles exist outside of each other—they do not completely overlap. Your job as a leader is to focus on the overlap. What is meaningful and doable based on the purpose, skills, market, industry, and resources available to the community. To be an excellent leader, you may need to place yourself within the community and without a leadership role. There, you may develop yourself into a leadership role.

Vision should be achievable within the five principles. From the outside, do-ability may be hard to perceive, so the leader must believe it is doable. While false bravado gets recognized, the result can be devastating.

Doubt. If ego is managed, doubt is next. Here are five areas to focus on for managing risk and doubt:

- Resource: If resources are limited, manage them carefully.
- Environment: Consider the environment and prepare to adapt to changes from perceived threats and opportunities.
- Market: Listen to the community, then adapt and change where you serve.
- Skill: Overcome your doubt by training.
- Purpose: Humbly, carefully, and continually articulate, reward, and protect the vision.

Incentive

Rooted in basic economics, incentive is important to working with communities. The highest articulation of vision comes through incentive. This is action behind words!

A community that desires any potential outcome must have incentive. This is true even for a community of one or two. Incentives are embedded in laws, policies, and culture. They are everywhere, and no incentive is universally bad.

Incentive comes in many forms—knowledge, recognition, opportunity, or resources like money or valuable items. For incentive to work, you must know your people. Some desire relationships, loyalty, or spirit-driven incentives. Others prefer money. Money is easy to quantify, but rarely hold the weight of loyalty, compassion, opportunity, knowledge, and recognition.

Bad incentives give poor results. Be simple, clear, and direct with incentive structures. Incentive structures that reward only individuals can cause unhealthy competition. Individual outcomes could improve with such incentive, but the overall community could diminish as competition prevents collaboration. The opposite can be true as well: incentive structures that award only the total outcome results in individuals letting others carry the full burden. Design incentive structure to allow motivation for individual and community skill, humility, truth, and self-sacrifice.

Massive incentive structures that require tracking dozens of outcomes are confusing and demoralizing. Individuals give up when faced with too many options. If you are under a complex incentive structure, weigh the overall structure. There may be dozens of outcomes, but they should all associate with some core components.

In business, core components may be sales, customer service, expense management, employee satisfaction, and operational efficiency. Each could have dozens of individual, trackable incentives or outcomes. However, this many measures can overwhelm. Instead, focus on one meaningful measure. Do that well, and the associated measures will also improve.

Organizations or communities with complicated incentive structures often reward one outcome more than the other. They may track and reward all outcomes, but the bulk of incentive rests in one core outcome. What this says is that people would be smart to focus on this one thing!

When you design incentive structures, have no more than five goals. This gives immediate clarity and meaning. It's also easier to understand and remember. As time passes, you can change or adapt incentives, but do not pile on new incentives. Remove and replace.

An ideal incentive plan rewards action, thought, feeling, and purpose. American President John F. Kennedy provided motivation for the first moon landing by giving all of America purpose, outlining necessary action and inspiring "new hopes for knowledge and peace" while detailing the mental hurtles and gains along the way.

Alignment is important in a business's incentive structure. Do your best to incentivize leaders, managers, directors, sales, operations, customer service representatives, and front-line people in the same way. Don't give bonuses for different successes. You may think it smart to do so, but it causes a mess.

The same need for alignment shows up in government as well. Leaders, politicians, citizens, and government employees should be incentivized in the same way. Congress should not get bonuses randomly. They should get raises when real wages rise.

People get nervous when the IRS or a police officer comes knocking. Why? Because they have different incentives. The police officer is probably incentivized to increase tickets, not decrease them. The IRS agent is motivated to collect additional taxes. (A job most IRS agents do quite well.)

Protection

Through punishment and disincentive, a community protects against the liar, trickster, and cheat. No incentive communicates a lack of priority or meaning. Decentralize leadership and allow community members to freely support and achieve the vision. Leverage unique ambition, skills, relationships, positions, and resources.

Of course, no incentive is perfect, and manipulation can happen. There will always be loopholes and bad actors. Humanity will subvert and pervert the most perfect of plans. There is power in working through that, but it is risky and that's okay. Skill develops only in the chaos of the unknown. Order stagnates. Yet absolute chaos is ruinous too. Balance between order and chaos. Do that with a "stick" and a "carrot" (disincentive and incentive).

Balance is, simply put, the least order possible to protect vision and incentive. Communicating a complex vision is hard, and a meaningless vision is meaningless. Simple is better. Apply this to protection as well. When possible, let the vision and incentive speak for themselves. Act only in the face of an intentional subversion of vision or incentive.

To achieve this in business, let people make mistakes, allow for problems and difficulty, and chase growth. At the same time, remove employees who are dishonest, have poor character, or take advantage of loopholes. Management guru Peter Drucker says, "The toughest decisions are people decisions: hiring, firing, and promoting people. They receive the least attention and are the hardest to 'unmake.'" The cost of having a bad actor is substantial. It is right to tolerate mistakes and differences, but not tolerate dishonesty or poor character.

In society, keep laws simple and allow people to make mistakes and determine the best path forward on their own. Let businesses go bankrupt and let people struggle. Never take from one group to give to another, and never take from an individual to give to a group.

> All men are created equal . . . they are endowed by their Creator with certain unalienable Rights, that among these are Life, Liberty and the pursuit of Happiness. (United States Declaration of Independence, 1776)

Only punish someone who takes life, liberty, or property from another.

Do not judge people as unworthy or incapable of living a meaningful life on their own. It is arrogant to think certain people are worth more than others. Who has the moral authority to judge a person as unworthy or unable of caring for themselves? Hospitals, nursing homes, not-for-profits, and religious organizations exist to help those unable to help themselves. You should give time, effort, money, and other resources to these causes, and government should incentivize this giving. If a community recognizes the individual's worth, it is appropriate to protect and reward this worth.

When you do not protect a vision and incentivize it from abuse, those who do not abuse the incentive get an obvious message: the incentive can be gamed, the vision is a lie, and the incentive is meaningless. This creates a run on the bank, abused benefits, bankruptcy, and moral decay.

PART III
PEOPLE

Chapter 8

KNOW THYSELF

People travel to wonder at the height of mountains, at the huge waves of the sea, at the long courses of rivers, at the vast compass of the ocean, at the circular motion of the stars; and they pass by themselves without wondering.

—Augustine

Who looks outside, dreams; who looks inside, awakes.

—Carl Jung

Understanding the Self

You are not here on this earth for your pleasure, but to serve. All major religions teach this. Even materialists observe this as structural in biology. You come into the world having to be served by others and you typically leave it in the care of others. In between, you live most of your life serving others. You find the most meaning when you give back, care for, and serve your community. People are important!

If you do not know people, you cannot provide service of any significance. As Stephen Covey wrote, "Seek first to understand." This is a cornerstone of quality leaders in government, business, and marriage. Yet one area of understanding supersedes all others, and that is where you start: understanding yourself.

Socrates taught that "The unexamined life is not worth living." He died for this belief, which makes it clear that such an idea, upon which Western civilization rests, should not be taken lightly.

In part I and chapter 2, you read about four key components of self (body, mind, heart, and spirit) and the importance of confronting physical, mental, emotional, and spiritual suffering to improve. It is imperative that you think of self and others as complete people. You may not beat another person, but do you treat their mental, emotional, or spiritual being as equal to yours? You may eat healthily and exercise, but do you care for your mental, emotional, and spiritual health?

It is common to consider people from a single angle, most often emotional or mental. People get labeled ignorant (mind) or crazy (heart), which is never good. When you give someone a bad label regarding one aspect of their being, it becomes easier to ignore their other aspects. Increased social labeling never has positive outcomes. Label the other side "crazy," and you can discount their "reasoned" argument. Call them "stupid," and you can discount their "emotional" plea. All people are body, mind, heart, and spirit. Treat people considering all of these, as that is how you want to be treated.

Start with yourself. Seek to know yourself physically, mentally, emotionally, and spiritually. In chapter 2, I discussed this, but a brief revisit is appropriate.

Body: Know your baseline of health and your physical abilities and strengths. Know the type and amount of fuel you need for optimal health.

Mind: Understand your psychological makeup, current position in life, and mental qualities you lack. Consider what you could learn and seek mental balance.

Heart: Emotional reactions that are logical such as desires and wants, can be controlled with the mind, but you have limited ability to control chemical-induced reactions influenced by your environment and physical makeup. Outside help can be beneficial in gaining perspective. Avoid addiction to emotional highs and lows, while accepting them as natural.

Spirit: There is more to you than consciousness; you are like an iceberg, with only part existing above the surface. Uncovering your spiritual self takes some digging. Ultimately, only God can fully reveal your spiritual self to you. Seek spiritual balance and do not feign animal innocence. Never pretend complete understanding over the spiritual.

Who Are You?

As a person, you have some things in common with other people. You need food, shelter, love, knowledge, and meaning. These are common across humanity, and you are drawn to commonality. That is why people discuss weather in an elevator.

When you get to know yourself, you pass judgment on your personality as influenced through time and space by its past and future, faults and virtues. If you are honest, you know you are not all you could be. In the Judeo-Christian tradition, this is known as acknowledging your fallen nature.

If you know your personality, this is a step toward understanding who you are in the present. Your ability to know yourself is packed with the grace you need to grow. Knowing the past's influence over you or understanding the impact of desires for the future grants wisdom for dealing with the self of today. Knowing your personality can provide a way to find commonality and to recognize differences from others.

Entire books about personality traits exist. In summary, they have this to say: Humans have unique personality traits organized into different groups within categories. There are introversion or extroversion, empathy, conscientiousness, drive, agreeability, and emotional stability.

You are a mix of many traits, but certain traits are likely stronger. Perhaps you are predisposed to anxiety, have heaps of self-motivation, or prefer to work alone. Your present personality type depends on your judgments of the past and desires for the future. You base personality on the degrees to which you judge and value emotions, knowledge, spirit, and the physical.

Ideally, you will balance between the comfort of order and the growth of chaos, with discipline and surrender mixed in according to your physical limitations. Your ability to balance all these determines your state of being. All traits combine positive and negative values; no trait is better or worse than another.

Interestingly, imbalance is both necessary and dangerous. The danger arises if you are blind to other less-dominant traits in yourself and others. Do this and you believe your personality type or trait is best. You risk corruption, as you allow subconscious tendencies to overcome balance (you cannot maintain "flow;" you miss the mark; you sin). No human has perfect balance. Therefore, to grow or leverage your abilities, you must either surrender or discipline your individual traits as you have ability.

By knowing yourself, you can understand your judgments and motivations. An active person should slow down and consider others. A thoughtful person should not neglect the time for action. The charismatic person should not dominate conversation but rather make a point to listen. The self-aware, empathetic person should care enough to realize results are important to relationships, and the analytical should make room for relationships in order to live more fully.

Understanding yourself helps know what motivates you. The more clearly you can articulate your psychological self, the better. Write about your personality! Write what makes you motivated or happy. Are these things tangible or intangible? Money, cars, and houses—or people, relationships, and meaning? What do you enjoy—solitary work or work in a team, as a leader or being led? Are you introverted or extroverted?

Next, note the positive and negative aspects of your dominant traits. Finally, write how you can mitigate these negative aspects and strengthen the positive. For bonus points, write ways to develop and understand traits that do not come naturally to you.

Time Travel

In the first section of this chapter, you were reminded of the four components of a person: body, mind, heart, and spirit. In the second section, you read about your present personality traits. In chapter 2, you read about building the self, which placed the cart before the horse. It is difficult to build yourself without knowing yourself. In steps the problem of time! But you must begin somewhere.

Start where you are. Use what you have. Do what you can. (Arthur Ashe)

You cannot know your limits until you find them. The first run, the first set of push-ups, and the first day of fasting reveal your limits. Just as with bodily limits, it takes work to discover the limits of other aspects of self—sometimes a lifetime of effort. It is often necessary to put action before planning or knowledge of self.

Action takes place in the middle territory. You act in the here and now, yet you operate within the parentheses of past and future. Action shapes who you are and what you will become. Many actions are outside your control. It is easy to fail on promises of a positive, good action. How many New Year's resolutions amount to nothing? Most. This is because action in the present is hard.

Your past influences you, and prospects motivate you in different directions. The danger is getting caught up in self-analysis, reflection, incrimination, and/or dreams. You often do not know what is important, harmful, or helpful until confronted with it. Never beginning means missing out on the chaos of the unknown and never addressing your past or envisioning your future.

As you stumble forward, it is hard to know what direction you will ultimately go, but eventually you may see a desired or undesired future. You may desire physical abilities, knowledge, relationships, and/or spiritual assurance.

Individuals weigh these components of self differently. Some value results or relationships, others recognition and legacy. For some, desires outweigh the possibilities perceived in the world. Others wish to avoid certain outcomes or components of self and therefore never face their full nature. Sometimes you think you know why you chose a certain path, and sometimes you deceive yourself. Sometimes you avoid parts of your nature for good reasons. Other times you choose for bad reasons and must return to your past to gain understanding.

The past can influence your character if you give it such power. You are a combination of nature and nurture. Some parts are intrinsic to your nature, others are developed, and some get developed so early they are essentially your nature.

What matters about your past is how you perceive it. When you were younger, you had less say about what happened. For this reason *why* is less important in the past because you cannot change it. *Why* answers your interpretation of an action. *Why* may determine how you tell your story of the past. Sometimes why you perceive the past a certain way is not apparent. When reviewing the past, seek to learn facts, or as close to them as possible. This helps you take responsibility for them today. Undoubtedly, others influenced you in the past, and you can take responsibility for that today. By seeking positive influences and rejecting negative ones, you take responsibility for your past today. Abused? Resolve today to not allow abuse to continue, to not perpetuate abuse, and to search for the means and methods to dictate a better story. This is learning from your past and not being subject to it.

There are important questions to ask yourself about your past. What happened in those pivotal moments that hold influence over you? Were they within your control, and why did these things happen? What can you do moving forward to create or avoid these situations? As you dissect your past, dictate what that past means today and what you want for your future.

You are your past, your interpretation of that past, and your desires for the future. Take responsibility for this. Take responsibility for your past, present, and future by dissecting it, writing it down, and analyzing it. As you write, your thinking may evolve. Dissect your life in writing. Review your strengths and weaknesses, desires and fears. Do this with the perspective of a body, mind, heart, and spirit paradigm.

People who write carefully about themselves become happier, less anxious and depressed and physically healthier. They become more productive, persistent and engaged in life. This is because thinking about where you came from, who you are and where you are going helps you chart a simpler and more rewarding path through life. (Jordan Peterson)

Chapter 9

UNDERSTANDING PEOPLE

God created mankind in his own image, in the image of God he created them; male and female he created them.

—Genesis 1:27 (NIV)

Adapt yourself to the things among you which your lot has been cast and love sincerely the fellow creatures with whom destiny has ordained that you shall live.

—Marcus Aurelius

Other People

It is not advisable to skip the "know thyself" requirement in the previous chapter. You have a set of unique traits and characteristics, and other people are unique balances (or imbalances) of traits and characteristics as well. Your knowledge of self limits your ability to understand people.

Sometimes it is easier to understand other people, but this mostly speaks about your ability to deceive and lie to yourself. Difficulty understanding others comes down to two core problems. First, you are more comfortable projecting onto other people, particularly those to whom you are closest. Second, the better someone knows you, the more they conceal things that make the relationship uncomfortable. This says more about you than the other person.

Without other people, nothing great, worthwhile, or meaningful is possible! Relationships are foundational. All religions, philosophers, and history drive this point home. In the Torah, God works through Moses; in the Koran, Allah works through the prophet; and in the New Testament, Christ calls all believers to discipleship. The foundational roots of Western philosophy are steeped in the Socratic method and dialogue. Cooperative, argumentative dialogue between individuals asking and answering questions to stimulate new thoughts and ideas is the basis of much of the world. No single man flew to outer space, built a skyscraper, or sailed across the ocean. It takes a team. Without understanding people, you cannot live a meaningful life.

Building relationships starts with valuing others. In business there is the "value chain." First described by Michael Porter, it lays out a framework for firms to create value through logistics, operations, sales, and service supported by infrastructure, management, technology, and procurement (M. E. Porter 1985). During the Industrial Age and the development of subsequent capitalist systems, value chains created prosperity for Western civilization. Accounting systems and physical structures developed around these chains. Now, there is a new value chain emerging—that of human value, a.k.a. employee relations.

As value chain systems become more efficient and effective, they increase the power of the individual! Musicians can now record on a computer, film their own music videos, and distribute their songs online. A few years ago, it took teams of people, a specialized recording studio, and corporate systems to produce and distribute a song.

Today, you have more freedom than ever before to focus on relationships. In the early twenty-first century, the transition from industrial to knowledge age was a struggle. That struggle continues onward to a relational age.

As more people reach their golden years, our conquering of much of the physical is apparent. Likely, you will die from old age instead of weather, starvation, or wild animal attacks, and you can comprehend the world better than past generations. A deeper understanding of your relationship to nature, the harnessing of energy, the functions of your body, and the constant breakthroughs in the neuroscientific understanding of the mind get laid before you too fast to keep up.

As the Knowledge Age matures and allows you to connect with others, you can transition to an age of relationships—if the center holds. While moving forward, remember that you are a physical being, and what you do not maintain physically manifests mentally, emotionally, and spiritually. Striving to harness knowledge and relational success is a worthwhile and achievable goal.

At their foundation, relationships are individual. The ideology of imago Dei (image of God) on which the modern age is built is primarily a relationship between self and God. Never place groups over individuals, dividing between haves and the have-nots, ethnicity, sex, or other factors outside a person's control. All are uniquely privileged and unprivileged, and all are blessed with a divine spark breathed into them at their creation. Place yourself over another individual, and you will cause division and find failure at every turn.

Success with others is valuing them. Valuing often results in a battle against understanding yourself and not putting yourself above others. It is also a battle to communicate your value to other people. It is easy to say "I value you." It is harder to communicate it in meaningful ways.

In the past, words were more valuable. Papyrus and parchment were difficult to get, so every word printed on them was pregnant with meaning. The value of the spoken word has fallen as well, but the cost of them has always been low. Learn to use words well so you can express your value and the value of others.

How to Value People

"I value you."

"You are a great _____." (person, friend, employee, and so on)

"I care about you."

"I love you."

The above means little when coming from me to you. They're mere words on paper—cheap, easily typed. It is easy to think that communications are about the right words, perfect grammar, correct diction, and the right presentation. While these things might communicate that I care about what I am saying, words communicate little about how much I care about you individually.

A husband tells his wife, "I love you." Does he communicate love? Does he know and understand her? Not perfectly. Consider this common trope:

> Behind every angry woman stands a man who has absolutely no idea what he did wrong. (All men everywhere)

Why is the woman angry? Because you can never know her perfectly. You are not inside her mind, you do not have the same experiences, and your synaptic connections formed differently. Therefore, communication is not only about words. Communication is about understanding. You will never understand another with words alone.

You must receive communication through listening. The excellent communicator is a good listener. Hopefully, the excellent communicator values other people and is not a manipulator. (Warning: It is preferable to be a poor communicator than a good manipulator.) Take time to listen to people, not for your benefit but because people are valuable.

Listening and Understanding

Most think listening is about hearing. But hearing is not listening. You hear music, but do you understand it? Do you know the individual notes? Is it in the key of D or G? Is it a simple 4/4 beat or something more complex? How does it change and move? Most people *hear* music. Few *listen* to music, and even fewer *understand* it. How much more complex is a human being than music?

Listening involves more than the ears. Of course, words matter, but how they say them matters more. Still more important are their actions. Listening is hearing what they say and how they say it, paying attention to mannerisms and body language, having situational and spiritual awareness, and observing their actions.

It's a given, but it is easier to understand people who speak the same language as you. Communicating is more challenging with social and cultural groups outside of your own. Educated elite speak differently than high school dropouts. But be careful—all types of communication are meaningful.

Speaking clearly is important if you value being understood. Simpler language is more inclusive but can be less descriptive. You will not always receive communication in a form that is ideal for understanding, and you can easily revert to "autobiographical listening."

If you value a person, withhold judgment of their words until you understand them. Avoiding "autobiographical listening" is about the intention to learn or judge. Withholding judgment until you understand is the wisdom of age and takes patience and maturity.

A second part of listening is clarifying. Clarifying is an attempt to reflect a person's words or feelings outwardly, showing confirmation that you understand the person. Simply summarize what the other person said and ask if you understand correctly. Often when you hear a person and become confused, you ask clarifying questions from your own perspective or analyze the other based on your experiences. As a result, you do not reflect the other person's words and feelings with the goal of understanding. Your self and your ego get in the way. This creates a negative feedback loop (usually emotional) of reverting to your own perspective. Next thing you know, your self and ego are on the line and you are unwilling to recognize it.

This does not mean you do not understand the situation. You may better understand the situation because of your outside perspective. However, you may misunderstand the other person's perspective and everything that informs it. Yes, the other person could be foolish or trying to intentionally mislead. However, determining motive is fraught with risks and indicates you do not value others.

You know you are listening well when you seek to clarify confusion. Valuing people and understanding them as resources is important, but valuing people is an end in itself. Reflect the other's position by summarizing their words. The more accurate your summary, the more empathy and understanding you have. When reflecting information to another individual, focus on what was said, the emotional content or feelings behind the words, the meaning or logic behind the communication, and the spiritual beliefs embedded in the communication. Keep in mind that communication may focus on a single area of their being. So, saying you are hungry does not necessarily communicate anything spiritual or emotional.

The following is an example of a reflective summary:

Thanks for sharing. You seem stressed by your work [reflecting physical perspective]. You feel unappreciated, and this takes a toll on your energy levels [emotional impact]. You really value your job and get meaning from it [content and logical/mental reflection], and this is a big deal to you [belief or spiritual reflection]! This makes sense to me, but am I understanding you correctly [clarifying question]?

Reflective listening with clarifying questions allows the other person to maintain ownership over their words. In the above example, the other person could reply with "Yes," "No," "Yes, but," "And," or other responses. Wherever there is an opportunity for clarification, practice reflective listening.

Keep in mind that clarification questions can be misunderstood as disrespect. If your reflective summary misses the mark, the other person may become defensive. Being patient, loving, and calm can smooth any offense raised by the reflective listening process.

How something is said envelops tone, emphasis on specific words, facial expressions, pace of speech, and the situation. When you seek to understand, you listen with ears, mind, eye, heart, and spirit. This was discussed in chapter 3, but here we are not relating but seeking to understand.

Tone or intonation is important. Music makes this obvious. Different tonal patterns communicate different emotional structures. Rock offers dissonance, blues and jazz lean on minor chords, and major scales match bright pop music. Musicians can mix tone to create complex emotional communication. The tone you speak with is just as important. To accurately reflect, listen and notice tone, both when you talk and when you listen to others talk.

One type of tone control is physiology. Your physical expressions manifest in your mind, heart, and spirit. A phrase like "How may I help you today?" said with or without a smile impacts tone. You can "hear" a smile, just as you can "hear" a frown. When you call customer service, you are quick to recognize if you will get help or not by "hearing" whether the person on the other end is smiling or frowning. Call a friend, and you can tell when it is a bad time to call. Light, amiable tones communicate, as do deep, dissonant, sharp, and flat tones. Mind your tone and the physiological connection to tone to communicate more clearly.

Emphasis also matters and can be verbal or nonverbal. By emphasizing words, you change the meaning of a phrase. "Do I understand you correctly?" Emphasize "Do," and the phrase implies burden or effort. Emphasize "I," and you come across as arrogant, the hero. Emphasize "understand," and you imply that the subject needs "understanding," which is easily interpreted as belittling. The emphasis belongs on "you." This communicates that you care about understanding the person.

Emphasis is nonverbal also. You understand a thumbs-up, eye roll, or middle finger. Other, less obvious nonverbal communication includes eye contact, body movement, nervous twitches, and more. Eye contact and upright posture communicate compassion and confidence. Lack of eye contact communicates confident disinterest. Slumped posture without eye contact causes the other person to question your ability to deliver on anything you say.

You can read people's nonverbal communication. Observe and study those around you to see what they emphasize when speaking.

Pace, which is situationally dependent, is another important facet of communication. Faster pace implies urgency. Slower pace implies relaxation, although it can also soothe in a crisis. By slowing your speech when someone is in crisis, they will likely mimic you to create rapport. However, this does not always lead to reflective listening, and such communication is situationally dependent. People want 911 operators and ER doctor to manipulate them toward safety and health. It is manipulative to control others' speech and emotions. Refrain from manipulating complaints or navigating away from tough conversations through nonverbal cues.

Situation matters, and you must take verbal and nonverbal communication within the situation's context. Important as it is, situational awareness is an imperfect art. It is often hard to understand an individual's situation. The person on the other side of the table could have had a bad day or experienced significant trauma. Your painful question only makes things worse.

People carry substantial baggage in their minds. Because of this, they give mixed messages. By minding the unknown, you can deal with others' unclear or garbled communications in a more meaningful manner. If you lock into your own situational view and circumstances, you will struggle to be mindful of others' situations.

The world is upside-down, and there is much of which you are unaware. A healthy paranoia about your wisdom and a mind of unknowns will help you be present in the moment. Such presence increases your situational awareness. Leave work at work and home at home to live focused and disciplined in the now. In this way, you will develop increased situational awareness where you grow your reflective-listening ability.

A Deeper Listening

Hearing is physical. You hear a sound and react. This flight-or-fight response ingrained into your being has helped our species survive. Only in the last 200 years has hearing decreased in importance.

For thousands of years, beasts of prey hunted your ancestors. There was a genuine need to listen and watch for changes in the weather— shifting winds, darkening clouds, and upturned leaves associated with changes in air pressure. Your ancestors' senses were necessarily attuned to survival. It was required in order to exist in a chaotic world that wanted to kill them. These facts get forgotten in our high-rise apartments, where we arm ourselves with protective devices and travel in armored vehicles.

Your senses protect you less each day. You now store information in books, pocket devices, and meta-cloud; you don't have to listen to every bit of information in nature to survive. In fact, you have the opposite problem: too much noise. Western civilization, the melding of reason and God's law, brought a spirit of common law that increases order and improves your ability to work with—as opposed to against—your fellow man. Occasionally, your acute stress response is useful, but it is rare and becoming rarer. Today's humans die from obesity, heart disease, and old age. Danger and evil still exist, but death rarely comes via a rushing beast or neighboring tribe. The new monsters are more complex. Will society continue down its path of growing informational order?

It is a blessing to live in an age in which you can slow down, control your reaction to acute stress response, and pause to listen to those around you. This is a new phenomenon you should strive to control. Your acute stress response, sharpened by evolution, may make trivial things seem biologically significant. You can trick yourself into thinking in a physical/biological sense and reacting in unhelpful ways. Perhaps you avoid conflict by running away, sit in fearful silence, or yell down a perceived threat.

Modern society grants the opportunity for growth when you control an emotional, mental, or spiritual reaction. This comes with disciplined, intentional effort, by seeking stress for growth and making mistakes. Again, mistakes are opportunities to identify weaknesses and improve your acute stress response.

The more deeply you listen, the more meaningful your relationships will be. Listening and withholding judgment is a relationship skill, the skill of the student (see chapter 6). Engage your mind and listen with your ears and eyes. And learn to listen with your heart and spirit.

How do you listen with the heart and spirit? Think of visiting the Vietnam Memorial Wall during Memorial Day weekend. Washington, DC, is crowded at that time, with veterans flocking to pay respects to their fallen brothers and sisters. The Capitol and monument fields are packed. There is a lot to hear. While approaching the Vietnam Memorial Wall, you step into silence. There, people speak in whispers, and children instinctively hush. It is easy to listen with the heart and spirit there, because those speaking at the wall do so with almost all heart. Their grief permeates the air.

Listening with heart and spirit reveals two voices: that of the person at the wall and that of the person whose name is inscribed on the wall. Pain, love, and a soldier crying at the wall all mean something. This is heart language. Spirit language is present as well. The wall speaks as a memorial of sacrifice. The wall itself is just marble and accounts for almost nothing. Its representation of a memorial that honors and remembers good deeds or learns from bad deeds of history is more valuable. Undoubtedly, the heart of the wall is heard in the stories of heroism, sacrifice, and pain, but these stories will fade faster than the memorial stone.

The memorial's spirit speech is dependent on the sacrifice. Sacrificing children for greed and a soldier sacrificing for their nation are different sacrifices. When you listen in the spirit, you can better perceive what is being said. Listen in the spirit of love, reason, grace, and truth, and you will see those spirits more clearly. Conversely, things of the dark side cloud reason and comprehension.

When forced to listen with your heart, you can sacrifice for your brother, home, or nation. The words at memorials echo the response of that ultimate language. You know this is true. It shapes the world. You hear it in those names on the wall who speak to you. Authors, poets, spiritual disciples, and philosophers speak in heart and spirit language as well. Listen.

Is war grotesque, dangerous, and barbaric? Yes, but there are things worth fighting for: justice, freedom, love, and all other good ideals.

Do not glorify war, but rather glorify the willingness to take a stand! Honor soldiers. There is no greater love than to lay down one's life for a friend. This is spirit language when spoken with meaning and leading to action. War and battle are not simply militaristic. Art is war. Arguments at work about right and wrong could be everything, and a disagreement with your spouse could be your salvation. Humbly letting go of what you value most—your self, addictions, and hopes—is a way of laying down your life for others.

Not every situation is Memorial Day in Washington, DC, or a personal battle. There is a deeper game you should recognize and be inoculated against. It is a winner-take-all game, a game for your being.

When you watch a movie and cry at the happy ending, you hear the sad or happy message, but do you grasp the inner meaning? The developed Western world is overstimulated by media designed to provoke emotional and mental reactions. Modern media is like a magician conditioning you to think a coin is in one hand while they hide it in the other. Media is software designed for your brain. By definition, its goal is to stimulate a response: increased attention and use, making a purchase, and so on. This may be a directly communicated offering or it may be hidden, which you pay for by watching an ad or sharing data.

Make no mistake: all media aims to influence the brain. Inoculate yourself by being conscious of it, disconnecting as needed, and disposing of unhealthy stimulus. Granted, this is easier said than done. Modern media designed by genius programmers and their AI is highly addictive.

If your heart feels stressed, worried, or sad about the latest bad news, how can you hear an act of love given quietly by your spouse? If your mind is engaged in zombie-surviving apocalypses, party music, and social media posts about the newest club, can you see your children's needs? Media feeds can be useful, but they become bad when they distract you from the here and now.

As algorithms and artificial intelligence progress in understanding the human mind, heart, and spirit, they become better at influencing your responses through individualized and targeted stimulus at deeper levels. The "game" is how effective programming can feed you emotionally stimulating messages and virtualized meaning that fill your desires. The prevalence of 24/7 news, social media, Hollywood, pornography, and gaming indicate these systems are succeeding.

Why do retail companies own newspapers and make movies and TV shows? Why is a social media company interested in virtual reality? There is big business in offering no value or meaning. Manipulating attention without value is peak inclusiveness and equity, peak success, "god out of machine" (deus ex machina), unlimited profits and power!

Hopefully, you're now awake, listen with your heart and spirit. Thankfully, people are rarely as manipulative as media and other groups. A fully integrated person will try and get close to speaking one message with body, mind, heart, and spirit. However, most speak disconnected messages—the coworker who holds animosity for years, the new boss who is uncomfortable with influence and power, the mom who is stressed with parenthood. It becomes easier to take stresses out on the world after a hard day at the office. It is hard to release the ego and admit failure. It is never easy for you to admit failures and stupidity. Expect others to have the same difficulty.

"I love you" can be delivered without action. If you expect action, does a lack of action overrule the words? Perhaps the missing action communicates that the other person is going through a mental, emotional, or spiritual struggle. Or maybe they lack energy to express fully what they say. When someone struggles with a disconnected message, listen more deeply. Value them, seek to understand, and clarify the confusion that exists between physical, mental, emotional, and spiritual.

People often live without intentionally integrated meaning and purpose. Their principles are not aligned. This is expressed in cries for help that may be silent, disconnected, and bumbling. When you hear this, you may hurt with the other person. Often all you can do is listen, and most of the time you cannot listen well for lack of practice.

It is one thing to *hear* the pain of the homeless, lost, sick, and dying; it is another to *listen* to it in all its painful detail. To those who listen to such people—first responders, counselors, pastors, doctors, and nurses—thank you! Burnout and mental health problems are common among those who specialize in listening deeply. Developing mindfulness, disconnecting, and practicing stress management are critical for those whose work requires deep listening.

Not all people realize they communicate with bodies, hearts, minds, and spirits. As you learn to understand other people and communicate better, you pick up on all that people communicate. Do not call people out on their inconsistent communications! It does no good to call out the frowning, beat-down customer service rep. When dealing with those closest to you, it is more serious. How does it help to call out a boss for not listening, a coworker for being insincere, or a spouse for sending mixed signals? There may be a time to point out these issues with loved ones, but precede cautiously.

Different cultures communicate differently. In the States, those in the North move at a faster pace and those from the South at a slower pace. Some cultures communicate emotional issues stoically, while others express emotions more openly. Different people, cultures, attitudes, and personalities all have unique ways of communicating. Different does not mean bad or good. True listening does not judge or confirm preconceptions.

Listening in spirit sounds vague because it transcends time and space. You can usually hear emotions by inflection in the voice, pace, and volume. Yet the spirit is a mysterious thing. The gospel of John states that the Holy Spirit is like wind: "Wind blows wherever it pleases. You hear its sound, but you cannot tell where it comes from or where it is going" (John 3:8 NIV). Listening in spirit opens you to the spiritual, a fearful thing indeed.

Sometimes this is stumbled upon. A person makes you uncomfortable, and you find out later that he was concealing something bad. Another person gives you a smile or pat on the back just when you needed it because she felt led to do so. Many misconstrue or ignore the spiritual. Don't be one of them. Listen for the spirit of truth and grace. When you find it, you will be well on your way!

Chapter 10

SOCIETY

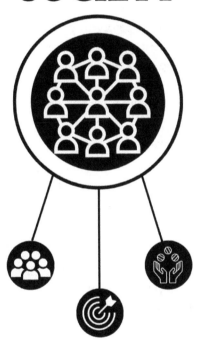

Let us think of ways to motivate one another to acts of love and good works. And let us not neglect our meeting together, as some people do, but encourage one another, especially now that the day of his return is drawing near.

—Hebrews 10:24–25 (NLT)

Propaganda works best when those who are being manipulated are confident they are acting on their own free will.

—Joseph Goebbels

Complexity

Individuals make up societies and communities, creating unique challenges. How does an individual or organization relate to a larger community, how do communities relate to each other, and how do communities relate to the individual? In health care, this is known as population management. Business calls it marketing. Government labels it propaganda. Religion deems it evangelization.

Two key points can be made about society. First, individuals are not always logical and are therefore unpredictable, particularly in large groups. For nearly a decade, political prognosticators have failed to predict election outcomes accurately, and no one consistently predicts the stock market's peaks and troughs. It is dangerous to listen to the masses and tailor your actions to their desires. Small amounts of populism and socialism are paths to ruin.

As the Chinese say, "When you ride a tiger, it is hard to dismount." You will fail in listening to the people, and unpleasant consequences will follow. Do not ignore people. Be mindful of selfish motives you bring into group situations and be transparent about your desires.

Second, the Information Age offers greater understanding of people. Communities can greater manipulate the individual and therefore the group. Communities that identify individual physical, mental, emotional, and spiritual shortcomings gain manipulating ability.

Often communities cannot see their own shortcomings or the consequences of artificial intelligence (AI) algorithmic processes. Yet the ability to feed these processes is growing. The ability for individuals and groups to self-actualize and integrate components of their nature and nurture is reaching new limits. This is in part good, but it is also dangerous. A desire for total inclusiveness, fixing everything and everyone, and finding a quick-fix formula puts people in God's position. Society has progressed so far and so fast that we have yet to fully comprehend what this means.

Power over the physical world allows manipulation of information, emotions, and spirit. Unfortunately, worldly power is not predicated on morality. AI systems do not require morality to use. Those left behind, unaware, and not principle-centered are at the mercy of complex manipulation campaigns. This is a testament to the power of reason and religion! As people turn toward love and justice, remember why turning matters: our fallen nature and need for God.

Seeing humans as physical, mental, emotional, and spiritual beings enables creators to design products and services that tap into all those desires. You are constantly managed, marketed, propagandized, and evangelized. Around each corner is another promise of spiritual, emotional, mental, and physical meaning, but these promises are rarely fulfilled.

Meaningful change requires sacrifice. Propaganda, platitudes, and marketing slogans cannot give meaning. Soldiers do not jump on grenades for their country; they jump on grenades to save their fellow soldiers. The individual leader who creates meaningful change and inspires meaningful change in others does it through self-sacrifice. Let go of ego, play the fool, point toward the shameful parts of yourself, and put your life on the line. Then you will change the world. Do this on your own, and you never let go of ego. You must allow God to work through you.

How can you promote and market honorably, and how can you counter marketing in your own life? Marketing can influence and recruit others into a new, better world. The more sincerely you market, the more honorably you live. Many view politics, business, marketing, and evangelism negatively. But they do not have to be. If you know what is meaningful and truthful and what helps confront suffering, share it!

The problem is that those seeking to influence others have little stake in the game. Can you sue media for the wasted hours of distracted attention? No, but everyday people get ripped off by media. Society is trading attention and wealth for nothing. With the rise of AI, this is becoming targeted, particularly to children and religious- and political-minded people. Shamefully, politicians and organizational leadership do not suffer for their wrong calls. Banks that default get bailed out, preachers who do not preach sacrifice get rich, and the gimmick weight-loss pill changes its name every six months and makes millions. Few live what they preach.

Marketing

Traditionally, *marketing* is a business term for communication intended to influence people to purchase. This definition is changing in our Information Age. As a result, governments, religions, individuals, health care providers, and schools now market. In their hands, the same goal applies: influence others.

Technology enhances marketing dramatically. In a world where physical survival is less pressing, society cares more for fun ideas and good feelings. Technology increases the speed and power of both, often obscuring the truth. For now, much of the West is being confronted with questions beyond survival. Marketing in all its forms is answering these questions, often by accident and incorrectly.

If you do not wrestle with the meaning of life, you are susceptible to finding meaning through the best marketer. A recent check of online retailer Amazon showed that thirty-two philosophy books on the meaning of life were published in a ninety-day period. For thousands of years, people either worked the field, hunted, and traded or died! New priorities beyond survival are a blessing, but society is ill-equipped to handle constant marketing. This provides a great opportunity for those with messages that are true and valuable.

Marketing capitalizes on a desire for the easy, safe, sound, peaceful, friendly, and good. Entry-level marketing recommends finding pain points and offering solutions. How does the product reduce suffering? Whatever you want to promote must solve a problem! The politician offers solutions, preachers provide answers, relationships bring value, and products offer benefits. The better you articulate how a given thing solves pain, the better you can market it. Religions provide solutions to the fear of death and the unknown; spouses and friends solve the pain of loneliness; schools and work provide knowledge, information, and opportunities for mental growth; and companies provide products and services to ease daily living through electricity, shelter, food, and more.

Sadly, people avoid pain. They avoid the doctor, dentist, tax man, life insurance salesman, therapist, and going to the gym or facing other unpleasant experiences. So, miracle drugs and easy ways out of hard conversations (social media echo chambers) sell by the billions.

It is hard (read: *painful*) to create something of true value, because meaning or value is best found in confronting suffering. The cost of creating a magic weight-loss pill that would let people live long, healthy lives is unimaginably steep. The temptation is to mislabel something and sell it as valuable—cheap grace, get-rich-quick plans, thirty-day methods to rock-solid abs, and becoming a master pickup artist. The gimmick is always short lived. It either does not solve the problem or covers up the symptom without addressing the underlying issue. The bigger challenge is creating or finding lasting value that addresses this underlying issue.

Once you have and articulate a solution to a problem, you move from entry-level marketing (articulating pain and solution) to market planning. Traditionally, business marketing included product, price, distribution, and promotion. The product may need adjustment to better satisfy the market, so you change the color, size, or scope. Modern marketing focuses on the demands of the consumer.

Three-dimensional (3D) printers can provide just-in-time inventories of custom-printed products, delivering flexibility to meet increasingly individualized desires. Proper pricing requires you consider the value consumers place on your product. Modern marketing focuses more on cost than price as consumers increasingly dictate what reaches production and at what price. A custom-designed laptop computer with key components individually selected costs more than a bargin Walmart laptop because of each customization.

Distribution determines how the consumer accesses the item—whether picked up at a particular location, sent through the mail, or delivered digitally. Modern marketing focuses on convenience as a key point for distribution, aiming to do whatever is easiest for the consumer.

Finally comes promotion. This is what the average person thinks of when they reflect on marketing. It is communication via advertisements. Modern marketing is becoming driven by consumers' desires and the marketer's ability to communicate how a product satisfies desires. You, your society, or community should articulate clear product, price, distribution, and promotion strategies that help share what is valuable.

The next step of marketing is research and segmentation to target specific groups or individuals. The internet and on-demand consumption of information allow companies vast access to individual habits. You have access to this information too. What people like to read, look at, and purchase; where they travel, what they do, and who is in their family mix; political and religious beliefs, and more help you drill down communication, product, cost, and convenience to specific groups and individuals. Once this data is compiled; consumers are analyzed; and price points, delivery methodologies, and communication strategies are articulated, the development of a marketing plan is well underway. But this is just a start. Marketing plans are in constant revision as the product or service goes through its life cycle.

Ultimately, the better you understand others' hopes, fears, and pain points, the better you can market your solution. If you have something of value, share it. A doctor who heals herself and not her neighbor, a musician who carries his great concerto to the grave, and a scientist unwilling to share her hidden knowledge are sad losses.

Sharing a thing has a cost for you, but it's worth it. Think carefully about how to price what you share. The exquisite artwork, engineering, and craftsmanship of a Ferrari have a commensurate monetary cost. Yet this is a small price compared to the cost of freedom paid on the battlefield and the cross. There is nothing bad about marketing and selling something of value.

A simple, incorrect solution is to sell or market something as cheap. In Michael Porter's *Competitive Advantage*, he discusses the competitive strategies of cost advantage and differentiation. Having the cheapest product does not guarantee success, the easiest sell is not always the best, and someone can come along and undercut a product. Purely competing on cost, then, is a losing strategy.

Cost reduction can undermine differentiation if it eliminates a firm's sources of uniqueness to the buyer. (Porter 1985)

You do this when you do not focus on things under your control. Cost is mostly outside your control. You become tempted to trade something for cheap when you do not put in the work outlined in chapter 8.

Have you fully invested your body, mind, heart, and spirit into what you are sharing? Consider the junk made in a Chinese sweatshop: it is not of high quality. The entire value chain focuses on greed, concerned primarily with cost. The quick path to wealth is to produce the cheapest product that you can sell at the highest cost. Greed is contrary to reason. The physical work is cheap, the heart of the product is greed, and the spirit of it will not last.

It becomes more personal when the thing being sold is an individual sharing a policy, belief, knowledge, or idea. This may be a politician who promotes only feel-good policies. It may be a preacher who does not struggle with theology or a teacher who does not question what they teach. Such items are naturally offered cheaply.

Cheap prices are not inherently bad; cost is a part of differentiation. You should care about delivering the best value possible. Price should not come at the cost of value and uniqueness.

Part of the problem with cheap things is the responsibility of the buyer. Hence, "Buyer beware." How you spend your money, time, attention, and emotional engagement reflects your value system. There is nothing wrong with laughing at a modern marketing campaign that over-promises to the point of absurdity, but it is disturbing how effective those advertisements are due to a society's value system.

The hallmark of good marketing is honesty. Shocking! The saying that "All marketers are liars" is not true. You must understand the product or idea and the target market. This is the hard work of chapter 9. Seek to understand others. A product's complexity and its market often dictate its value. But complexity does not always equate to value. Simplicity is often more valuable and cheaper to produce; however, making something simple can be complex.

Always undersell and over-deliver. Never promise something you cannot deliver. Granted, this is easier said than done, and a competitive landscape makes this more challenging. Keep a margin of error to keep your integrity intact. Be honest with where you are in the competitive landscape and the value you provide. This honesty takes humility and courage.

Honesty in marketing might translate to fewer initial sales, but people will value your influence. Honesty pays dividends via referrals and long-term customers, relationships, influence, and meaning. As a marketer and a human, integrity is one of your most valuable assets.

How do you honestly communicate solutions for people's pain points? Know yourself and seek to understand others. These help you relate through story. Aesop's fables display a story's power to contain distilled truth. There was no historic conversation between sheep and wolves, but the moral of being wary of helping those who want to destroy you holds true. A good marketer tells a story that shows the truth of a product or idea without the story necessarily being historical. Just be careful. Good storytellers can disguise stories as real and true, even when the story is neither. Do not do this.

Good marketing stories resonate emotionally without manipulating. This allows you to follow emotional connection with logical information. People purchase emotionally and justify logically. This is good marketing.

The last aspects of marketing deal with handling the objections of affordability and meaning.

Affordability is financial, but it also takes ability, time, and desire into consideration. People often desire and value contradictory things. Affordability is assessing whether something is more valuable than the thing being shared. If you value money more than the cost of a car, the money stays in your bank account. Skilled marketers make affordability a nonissue, which is dishonest. When affordability is a nonissue, the marketer is lying.

The most common issue, particularly with items of high complexity, is knowing how to value them. Do this by being honest about the cost, the effort taken in acquiring, and the need or desire being filled. If a person has no need, no resource, and no ability to purchase, move on.

No need, resource, or ability means the lesson of knowing yourself and understanding others is missed. The consumer simply made an assessment and deemed the thing was not affordable. If possible, ask why the item was deemed unaffordable. A good marketer or salesman learns from this, adds value, tweaks the product, reworks the idea, or returns to the drawing board. However, the more accurately you provide information on need, cost, and effort, the more likely someone will know upfront whether they can afford it.

Your goal is to avoid someone not knowing if they want what you are sharing. There are some excellent resources for dealing with negotiating, selling, and marketing, which are in the resources section of TheFivePrinciples.com. It is easy to think of these from a business perspective, but they permeate all of life.

Lastly, what you market and sell should point to meaning. Everyone buys junk, like a souvenir mug at a theme park. It has meaning in the moment, but then it is gone. The meaning was in the activity, and no piece of junk brings that back.

At the dawn of the twenty-first century, we are in a marketing free-for-all. As culture becomes more focused on the material and less on the spiritual, emotional, and mental, actions become easier to manipulate. The desires of hearts are replaced with things, knowledge with wisdom, and self in the place of the spiritual. A world filled with physical and knowledge abundance that lacks wisdom and emotional control is ripe for meaningless marketing.

Gurus, magic health pills, and instant wealth sell billions through manipulation. Instead, communicate what is truly meaningful. Reject that which does not have meaning or promotes a lie—the sugar-loaded fake news, imaginary lover, garbage products, and social media manipulation.

Counter Marketing

Survival is hard. Yet the desire for the easy path is strong. Marketing gimmicks claim all your problems will get fixed if you just buy this thing. They provide access to the easy path.

It is easy to forget the thousands of years of evidence that survival is a struggle. The weak, sensitive, ignorant, lost parts of you want the easy path. When you get caught up in modern living, you are most susceptible to forget the physical challenge of surviving, the work that relationships and knowledge take, and the importance of the spiritual. This generation has fought no great wars, lost the war on terror, and embarrassed itself with the drug war. It is the end of Pax Americana. There have been no great cataclysms, aside from a pandemic. It is the calm before a storm, but most people do not notice the age coming to an end.

As discussed previously, one of the golden rules of marketing is to identify pain and provide a solution. Thousands of years ago a slave rose to power and enslaved the entire nation that purchased his slavery. This is one of the greatest examples of marketing in human history—a confident young man claimed a vision and marketed that vision until people bought. They enslaved themselves to his vision because they allowed the slave to do the work. Joseph, sold into Egyptian slavery, marketed himself as having special insight from God. He could protect Egypt from potential famine, and he made it easy for those he would protect. Eventually all of Egypt was in debt to the government led by Joseph. Joseph shows how to handle challenges, follow God, stay true to your beliefs, maintain honor, and rise. His story also teaches to be careful about what power you give others. Joseph could save his family and a nation, but the nation and Joseph's family paid a steep price for their salvation.

Modern marketing has two key problems. Carelessness leads to problems being solved that do not benefit people. And, by making things too easy, the amount of discipline required to stay on the path is increasing.

As a group, humankind is just learning to survive. The jury is still out on whether this is a short-term fluctuation or a permanent, sustainable trend of progress. The last eight thousand years of history do not provide evidence as to the previous seven hundred thousand of Homo sapiens evolution. America's two-hundred-year experiment in freedom and self-government does not prevent the world from returning to rule by authoritarian regimes.

HumanProgress.org provides evidence regarding the progress of humanity and our well-being.

Only now has humankind learned

how to push the limits of our limited life expectancy. By living with an abundant supply of nutrition and medicine in a society getting better at existing within earth's hazards, humankind now regularly survives birth, youth, and middle age. Because our existence outside of fighting for survival is new, we cannot understand the importance of losing this fight.

What would be lost if a pill expanded life expectancy by hundreds of years or more? What if you could put off facing your own mortality? We are nearing a time when these will be legitimate questions and not science fiction. Knowing you will die forces you to search for meaning. In Judeo-Christian theology, God's first act of mercy and grace is forbidding humankind to eat from the tree of life. Your fight for survival is important, and society needs more of it. Having everything on demand is not healthy. What happens when there are no grocery stores, the supply chain is limited, and the utility grid crashes?

Silk sheets, soft beds, delivered food, luxury vehicles, happy and skinny pills, diets, climate-controlled gyms, and ubiquitous entertainment are but a taste of modern convenience. Most are good in the right circumstance and with moderation. Balance, however, is hard to obtain. Finding it is an individual struggle that starts with being aware of the need for balance and then seeking that balance that best serves your physical, mental, emotional, and spiritual beings.

The second problem is that humankind does not know the limits of mind, heart, and spirit. Few people actively push the limits of their minds, fewer their ability to love and relate, and fewer still strive to obtain transcendent spiritual living. This leaves space for marketing to fill and engage with the softest media notions of comfortable, mindless, zero-truth, feel-good nonsense.

You must work to create quiet spaces to contemplate and do real thinking—a battle against communication device notifications, for sure! It is a fight to make time for contemplation. On average, the smartphone user completely wastes two days on their phone a month (Kommando Tech Statistics on Phone Use 2020), and that number is rising as artificially intelligent super algorithms improve a device's abilities to capture attention.

Humanity is sold not *why* but *how* to live. Yet it is not *how* you live that matters. It is meaning beyond yourself, *why* you live that gives you meaning. Your legacy—your spirit, at least—lives on in the art you create, what you build, the ideas you defend, and the God you worship. Do not allow noise from the community to distract you from all you were created to be! Seek a community that encourages freedom of real, quiet thought.

To counter marketing, be careful how you spend your money, give your attention, invest your emotions, and build your legacy. Marketers who promise simple solutions for daily living—get rich quick, lose weight in seven days, find the perfect mate, or receive cheap grace—must be countered with discipline, focus, and purposeful living. High-carbohydrate foods, weight-loss pills, pharmaceutical cures, Match.com, and megachurches are massive industries because humans are new to this soft way of living.

You will make mistakes. You will fall for gimmicks and fads. Reduce your gullibility by increasing your awareness. Be hesitant about things that make life too easy. Ask how the quick fix fulfills your purpose, builds discipline, and creates space to focus on real development of body, heart, mind, and spirit. Automobiles make travel easier and increase your ability to find more challenging work, get home more quickly, or escape your local community to experience a larger world. A more luxurious vehicle could allow you to arrive at your destination more refreshed and engaged, but do not get caught up in diminishing returns. Whatever the thing is, it should bring you more meaning, not less.

In a time in which messages get delivered in visual, audible, and dynamic ways, skepticism is increasingly helpful. Marketers can design messages of increasing influence that are more and more specific to smaller groups of individuals. Social media tailors' ads by leveraging powerful AI algorithms. You are literally competing with robots for your own conscious attention—and regularly losing. Supermarkets can identify customers who are pregnant, often before family knows, and market items directly to expecting mothers. In the future, 3D printing and digital design will permit you to subconsciously design your own products! One day soon, designer drugs for your specific DNA traits could hit the market. These are impressive. The ability to abuse and sell meaningless things to people in various physical, mental, emotional, and spiritual states is just as impressive.

Keep your life simple, be skeptical, and keep your focus on what is meaningful.

PART IV
ENVIRONMENT

Chapter 11

YOUR WORLD

Resolve to know the laws of nature, follow them in all circumstances, let them shape you, be guided by their perfect wisdom.

—Epictetus

God, grant me the serenity to accept the things I cannot change, courage to change the things I can, and wisdom to know the difference.

—Reinhold Niebuhr

Things Outside Your Control

Most of this book has been about things within your control. Part IV transitions to dealing with things outside your control—the environment in which you live.

You live in a different world. You were born into a different time, culture, geography, and family. Even if you are a twin, you have a unique mind. As society becomes more homogeneous, we risk viewing differences as fairness or unfairness, haves and have-nots, you versus them. But life is not about comparing yourself to others; it is about doing good with what you have.

You waste effort when you compare yourself to others because you have different opportunities and challenges that are largely outside of your control. In fact, lack of control and the extremity of differences are the two biggest similarities between people. Focus not on others, but on who and where you are, in the here and now.

Just because something is outside of your control does not mean it is unimportant. It is important in a stoic sense—not in your ability to change your environment (although this is possible) or to have irrelevant criticism of your environment (although you can criticize it). Rather, it is important as it enables you to recognize and accept your environment for what it is. You must understand and accept your environment, then seek to understand the environments of those with whom you have meaningful relationships, and finally, understand the greater environments of organizations and communities with which you interact.

Part II discussed strengths and weakness internal to you, your relationships, and your community. Weaknesses can be mitigated and strengths improved upon. With external opportunities and threats, you may adapt, capitalize upon, or mitigate them. Your ability to assess, accept, and plan for how you will adapt to your environment is critical to survival and your ability to carve meaning out of the world.

Because pain strongly influences people, you risk learning to avoid pain to survive. If companies, media, religions, and politicians told you everything was good, you would not need to buy their products or listen to them.

You are a problem-solver. When others tell you the problem, you latch onto it. In the primitive jungle, if you see someone running and wait to verify what they are running from, the tiger will eat you. Today, you are not in a primitive jungle but in an increasingly more informational, relational, and transcendent jungle. Have you developed the natural tendencies to recognize the logical, emotional, and spiritual "tigers"? Humankind is barely into the Information Age and is a long way from an emotional age, much less a spiritual age. Will humanity make it out of the Information Age without knocking itself back a few centuries? If so, what will a truly emotional or spiritual age look like?

Be careful about listening to people who tell you the type of world in which you live. Look and judge for yourself. As you do, remember that your eyes lie. For example, the sun does not revolve around the earth although that is how it is perceived. You have biases. Even your environment influences you.

To understand your environment, understand yourself: your past and present, strengths and weakness, and vision for the future. The work in chapter 8 is a prerequisite. By recognizing your biases, you are better able to mute biases from your analysis of the world. Despite this, you will never perfectly see the world as it is. To realize this, let go of ego.

In stoicism, this is the Discipline of Assent. You perceive the world around you, form a snap judgment, present it to yourself for consideration, and make a judgment. When you judge an item, you have three choices. The item is either good, bad, or requires more consideration before being labeled.

Your ability to judge correctly goes back to the questions from part I: is it meaningful, does it serve people, and does it align with nature or God? The stoics referred to this as *logos*, the physical laws that established order in the cosmos and permeate all of nature. This "word/logos," lived out in the person of Christ, expounded on by the apostles' writings and letters to the church, and carried through time by saints, is the perfect example of this. These two schools created the pillars of reason and faith on which Western civilization rests.

What environmental influences do you allow into your life that influence you, threaten your way of seeing, or give you opportunity to improve? As poor diets, poor exercise advice, worthless information and entertainment, cheap pleasures, and spiritless interactions increase, so will blindness and deafness. You may not control your environmental influences, but you can identify those to avoid. Listen to your teachers and bosses, but beware that which does not align with God or nature, help your fellow man, or give life meaning.

Your jobs may require connection to environmental influences (government, bosses, coworkers, media, etc), and those with whom you have relationships may wield environmental influence (friends, spouses, etc). You cannot completely disconnect from your environment, so seek to develop a deeper awareness of environmental influences. This requires discipline to create a space where you can control what noise can influence you. This helps you assess your environment and better yourself without manipulation from outside voices. Often, outside influences signal about environmental factors outside of your control and influence that are irrelevant to why you live your day-to-day life in a particular way. As you gain discipline in managing the influence of outside voices, you will become better at hearing the truth.

In *The 7 Habits of Highly Effective People*, Stephen Covey writes about circle of concern versus circle of influence. Your circle of concern is larger than your circle of influence; concern can include your whole world, anything that might concern you. Your influence does not extend past what you have control over. If you confuse these two paradigms, you will spend your energy on things outside your control. To expand your influence, deal with things under your influence: spirit, heart, mind, body, room, home, relationships, work, and communities. Dissect your environment. Writing your perceptions of the environment is great for thinking through your world. You can find meaning as you consider your environment from a physical, mental, emotional, and spiritual perspective; however, as you move from the tangible to the intangible, it becomes harder to discern.

As you assess your environment, the first hurdles you must overcome are ego and bias. One way to notice ego and bias is identifying emotional reaction. When this happens, you are under the environment's control. Such emotional response is natural, but you do not have to accept it. Should a serious injury happen, the calmer person who accepts the situation has a greater chance of survival than does someone who panics. In martial arts, the first lesson is how to relax in stressful situations. Until you learn calmness under pressure, you cannot learn much else.

As you look at your surrounding environment, assess and accept opportunities, threats, and unknowns. Look for opportunities to build your being and threats that promise to tear you down. If you make a home secure and ordered without emotional attachment, you are blessed. Of course, you can make your home secure and ordered only if you can make your mind secure and ordered. If you can create an ordered, secure home, you can build meaningful relationships in which you can assess and accept those around you for who they are.

With an ordered home, meaningful relationships, and work that builds your intellectual abilities, you can align yourself with the spiritual environment around you and influence the past* and future.

All people have different environments. Living in a world of peaceful abundance versus one of wartime loss and strife manifests in different assessments. A jungle missionary environment is dramatically different from that of a Wall Street hedge fund manager. *Assess* and *accept* stay the same, but the opportunities and threats become as different as night and day. A jungle missionary living in a simple hut, who is in sync with his wife, and learning a tribal culture and teaching simple religious truths may touch the spiritual more quickly and easily than those caught up in a material, informational world.

Before viewing threats and opportunities as bad and good, remember that the unknown exists, and you can always withhold judgment until you get more information.

When you align with the spirit of truth, correct assent/judgment at a spiritual level, you influence the past by changing your perspective on the meaning of the past. You choose the stories you tell about the past. You choose what meaning, significance, and influence the past has over you. You can take a past tragedy, and it can be a story of brokenness; or you can take a past tragedy and make it into a story of healing.

Threats to Being[*]

What threatens being? More directly, what threatens your physical being, mental being, emotional being, and spiritual being?

Threats to Physical Being

For you to have purpose, you must survive or—better—trade your life for something meaningful. In modern society, threats to daily survival are reduced. This does not mean these threats do not exist or cannot return. Today in the United States, about 1 in 250 people will experience violence, such as murder, rape, robbery, or assault. (Staista Research Department 2021) This is a low rate, although not the lowest in the First World. New Zealand, Iceland, Japan, Austria, and Norway have the lowest.

Given the consequences of such an encounter, there is benefit to mitigating the extreme consequences of a violent encounter. Basic physical fitness, self-defense, and firearms can be the difference between life and death. For anything statistical with a non-ergodic outcome (think Russian roulette), be careful at drawing conclusions. Survival training can come with other physical, mental, emotional, and spiritual benefits.

At certain times in history, the number of violent deaths (not just violence) exceeded one in ten. The Our World in Data organization provides analysis of long-term trends in violence. The hope is that these trends continue toward the positive, but there is never a guarantee, and society and culture go through cycles.

If the world resets the systems of order and justice currently in place, what will the consequences be? On what will people base new laws and rules? Feel free to withhold judgment on what this means, while still preparing for potential threats.

Keep in mind that this analysis is substantially based on time, place, and circumstance. It is written in the twenty-first century in a wealthy, developed country from the perspective of an educated individual capitalizing on the opportunities of such a world. Any analysis and discussion of threats will be limited, but the exercise, thought process, and analysis can still be valuable either from what is not known and proves not to work through history or what applies in a timeless manner.

Most likely, you do not harvest, hunt, or raise your own food, and you probably did not build your home. You rely on a complex supply chain to provide resources for daily living, each delivered with efficiency and complexity. As other countries join the power of a democratic market and liberated world, they taste the fruits of liberty too. Do they want to pay the price for freedom, and will the Western world continue to pay the price to maintain complex supply chains?

Physical fitness is a basic reaction to an assessment of potential challenges, since the labor of hunting, farming, and fixing your own shelter is no minor matter. Be able to care for yourself. The biblical story of Joseph shows the consequence of not setting aside for potential famine is slavery. Society should invest in infrastructure—not faux infrastructure. The West buys cheap junk and consumes large quantities of empty calories, media, relationships, and information.

The largest physical threat is existential. The religious believe God created us as bodies, and the nonreligious believe you are only a body. Your physical existence carries meaning regardless of religious belief.

What threatens you if you are physically spoiled? What do you lose when you become accustomed to pleasure? How easily can you forget what living healthy feels like? The pleasures of sweet food, carbs, comfortable chairs, on-demand entertainment, pornography, climate control, alcohol, drugs, "free" education, and modern medicine can trick the being into forgetting the importance of the physical. Our environment masks our fragility, weakness, ignorance, and immaturity as we pop pills, drive cars, and hop online.

Is this as an existential threat or an opportunity for your physical being? Perhaps an answer lies in society's suicide rate, which is approximately twice as high as the murder rate.

Threats to Mental Being

The Information Age inundates you with more information than you can comprehend. Society knows more, but you know less in relation to the knowledge available to you. Because of this, one of the biggest threats to your cognitive ability is inability to focus.

There are limited hours to learn. If this age fills your mind with sports scores, TV shows, pop lyrics, political news, or other trivial content, how can you cram in anything useful? Besides cultural distractions, there is the mental cost of your work. More and more work demands more mental resources; this is great if you do mental work that builds your being, but this is not always the case.

Thankfully, your mind is like a muscle. The more you exercise it, the more you can engage it. The more you build it, the more you can build onto it. I suspect your cognition limit is beyond what can be imagined. There are long-term, upward trends in human intelligence. An excerpt from "Are We Getting Smarter?" in *Scientific American* implies that you are living in a time with a broader range of cognitive problems than your ancestors encountered. In response, you have developed new cognitive skills and brain power. Comparing MRIs from 1900 to 2000 shows an increased thickness in neurons that are predicative of enhanced IQ performance (Flynn 2020). The difference between being overloaded with useless information and interacting with beneficial information is focus. Information is useful when it builds or improves your ability to solve cognitive problems. The more you assess active threats to your cognitive health and capitalize on opportunities to develop your mind, the more your brain will benefit.

Be careful about what you let into your mind. For the last few centuries, our education systems have improved, access to written knowledge has increased, and computers have dispersed information with newfound ease. As the cost of information distribution plummeted, the value of information did as well. It is not reasonable to assume that accessing cheap, valueless information will continue to enhance humanity's cognitive ability.

More than anything you guard, protect your mind, for life flows from it. (Proverbs 4:23 CEB)

Be disciplined with your focal systems—visual, auditory, and tactile.

Writing engages all of these. Listen to the voice in your head or to your teacher, visually focus on words you write, and engage your tactile systems while writing. Smartphones do the opposite of this, hijacking all three focal systems with 4k screens, Bluetooth audio, and infinity touch screens! The price you pay for these devices is focus. The information flows like a fire hose and is difficult to balance.

Mind and body are connected. A last threat to cognitive ability correlates with body. Physical fitness and proper diet impact cognitive ability. Succumb to physical threats and expect to roll over in the face of mental threats.

Threats to Emotional Being

Mental and physical weakness threaten emotional being. You see this when a family's breadwinner loses their job and the addictive nature of governmental help eats at them. Relationships come apart. As the environment increases influence over body and mind, it affects relationships and mental health. Mental health is not fixed. You do not experience peak mental health every day. You must work to protect it. What you choose to care about affects your emotional health, and it is human to care deeply.

Knowing the difference between areas of concern and areas of influence is helpful. If you place something outside your control in a position of influence, it will have power over you. Clinging to what is outside your control can cause painful emotions. As a human, attachment is part of life, but you must accept things as transient and outside your control, thus mitigating their threat to your emotional well-being.

Taking responsibility for your emotional or mental health falls in the realm of behavioral health. When you take responsibility for your choices and behaviors, you can improve your mental health. You cannot control the surrounding environment; it will always be a threat. You can, however, take responsibility for attachments and behaviors and therefore, your emotions.

From a student, teacher, and partner perspective, students depend on others; teachers are mostly independent; and partners are interdependent, their relationships creating synergy. There is a paradoxical balance here, as the most powerful relationship is the interdependent, synergistic partnership. Yet the most important relationship is that of the student, which is dependent on the environment to learn and grow. When you choose to be a student, you place yourself in a vulnerable place where judgment falls on you. It is also a place where you can grow.

However, if you always remain a student—always taking, never teaching, and never partnering, you remain dependent on others, like a child. Grow up! Good parents want their children to become adults, your spouse wants to be married to an adult, bosses do not want childish employees, and schools want graduates. Never advancing from dependence to independence to interdependence sabotages relationships.

Lessen threats to your emotional health by growing stronger in your independence from others where possible. Recognize the balance in this, and accept and take responsibility for weaknesses. Be careful of the dichotomy; you will not be content as a forever student, but you cannot grow without humbling yourself as student. This is a constant cycle.

Luck and grace have allowed you to navigate the threats in your life thus far; be humble and caring for others. For while many navigate the storms of life, many do not fare so well and are in need.

The biggest emotional threat to mental health is other people. It does no good to get upset at weather, math, scientific equations, or facts outside of your control. Storms happen and facts are facts. If you take responsibility for your choices, you probably recognize your emotions are about your failure to know the facts beforehand, just as if you were unprepared for a storm.

It is different when dealing with people. You know yourself somewhat, and you think others should act with logic that you understand. It is easy to confuse other people's actions as intentional actions against your desires—especially if the person is close to you.

There are two ways to deal with mental health threats coming from other people. Start by not allowing your mental health to be influenced by people who do not care about your mental health. Weigh a relationship's potential emotional damage against the amount of emotional desire you spend on such relationships. Being aware of these balances can help modulate your desires and expectations. Second, once you take responsibility for your mental health, protect the weak. If you are mentally strong, teach others. If you are emotionally stable, love people.

Caring for others' emotional health is a serious matter. If you care about people and you want people to reciprocate, put in the emotional work. This requires taking a real-world risk with your emotions. The benefit is that if you have a strong network of people who know you care about them, you probably have a strong network of people who care about you. As hard as you work to protect your emotional and mental health, there will always be threats to it. Being interdependent is therefore superior to independence. You may get back up after emotional blows, but it is easier and quicker with someone by your side. A person with strong family, friends, and community connections is emotionally stronger because of those relationships.

Be careful not to take emotional responsibility for others. You cannot control others' emotional states, but you can influence them, and you should care about them. Be responsible for what you say and do, but if you accept responsibility for how others feel, you can become overwhelmed by the other people's pasts, strengths, weaknesses, and desires. Worse, if you take responsibility for someone's emotions, you rob that person of responsibility for their emotional state. Never make people emotionally dependent on you. Emotional dependence forms an unhealthy power dynamic, the Oedipal/Electra complex written about by Freud in which the "devouring mother/father" becomes overbearing and brings about complex psychological issues by not allowing their children to develop independence.

In the last chapter, you learned to influence people with emotional language and how to counteract this. Emotional arguments, claims, and marketing are powerful tools to influence people. Strive to communicate and influence in emotionally truthful ways. Lessen the impact of those who seek dishonest influence, and be wary of those communicating in emotionally untruthful ways. Ask whether the motive of the influence seekers aligns with that of the influenced? Honesty and simplicity create transparency of motive; where motive hides, tread carefully.

Threats to Spiritual Being

Inability to relate, think, and act shows you have little with which to impact a tangible, orderly world. You are a feather on the wind—devoid of meaning. This is a lie. You are a self-aware being who can grow and adapt to the wind. You can build a sail to change your direction in relationship to the wind. You exert influence and control over your physical, mental, and emotional world. In the same way, you influence the spiritual world; you can have a legacy, which exists outside of time and the physical, logical, and emotional world.

The main threat to your spiritual being is meaninglessness. Whatever insists that the stories of the past and future have no meaning threatens your spiritual being. They threaten your ability to make sense of today. They threaten with despair and hopelessness, leaving you with a feeling that nothing you did mattered and nothing you do will either. These threats tell you that random chance brought about your awareness of death, your creative and artistic nature, and your consciousness. When you repress and do not confront your failings, you threaten your spiritual being by denying meaning in your life.

The spiritual exists outside and inside you, because it is separate and integrated with your other states of being. C. S. Lewis wrote, "We do not *have* a soul—we *are* a soul; we *have* a body." The things that are often most important are intangible—love, spirit, intellect, and will. The stories you tell about your environment give the outside environment meaning. The wind is the wind, but what you tell yourself about the wind matters more than the wind itself. How you assess and adapt to the environment is more important than the environment, because you create meaning by assessing and adapting. Therefore, the biggest threat to spiritual being from the environment is not the environment. It is you.

This may seem contradictory, but just as the environment is outside of your control, your subconscious is substantially outside of your control as well. In Judeo-Christian religious belief, this is the sin nature. The apostle Paul wrote in his letter to the Romans, "I do not understand what I do. For what I want to do I do not do, but what I hate I do" (Romans 7:15 NIV). Modern psychologists call this our "id" (Freud) or "shadow self" (Jung). Your unconscious nature is being driven by instinct, desire, and need, living largely outside your control. Pleasure motivates it in hopes of finding instant gratification.

When you question why you ate a certain food, slept in, skipped a workout, lied, drank too much, or turned away from that challenging activity, you succumbed to your unconscious sin/id/shadow desires. In Jungian psychological terms, you have not fully integrated your being—unconscious (sin/id/shadow) with conscious. In religious terms, you are following not the Spirit of God but the spirit of self. It is common to repress the shadow self or deny sin nature.

Science does not understand consciousness and subconsciousness. It makes people uncomfortable and is commonly projected onto others. The worst is to give in to it and allow it control, to follow your passion and do whatever feels good.

When you integrate the unconscious self, you can rewrite the stories you tell. This is dark work that requires you to confront unpleasantries. Strivings brought on by anger, envy, desire, selfishness, and greed are natural. Maybe you feel envy because you want to be better, you are greedy because you want to store up for the future, or you are righteously angry because of injustice. You cannot control your impression; what matters is whether you assent and how.

Is it right to envy wealth when you sleep in or health when your workouts lack? Yes, if you recognize your role in the difference and therefore improve; no, if you use it to justify jealousy and resentment, treat others badly, or tear down what they have. Once you recognize your sin nature, the challenge is integrating it. This is deep spiritual work and outside the scope of this book. It is important to note some key risks up front. There is risk of sin/id/shadow work ending in possession. If you allow this nature to rule you, you can spiral into chaos. Also, it is not just repressing it. If you deny sinfulness, it may emerge when you are not expecting it—the white lie leads to a big lie, which leads to manipulation, hurting others, and covering up at all costs.

Psychologists encourage balancing the walk between possession and repression toward integration. They do not fully grasp the importance of the spiritual in this work, but I respect the modern language they use to describe the problem. I believe the only way to integrate this nature is by following the one who perfectly integrated spiritual and fleshly nature by putting himself on the cross so you may be born again.

If the biggest threat to spiritual being is your subconscious, the saddest threat to spiritual being is allowing others to dictate the stories you tell. Deal carefully with the impressions others make and judge them as worthwhile, worthless, or lacking information before acting. This is a struggle, but you are responsible for where you are and the story you tell.

Be wary of lies encouraging you to embrace your shadow/id/sin and give in to pleasure and meaninglessness, to eat, drink, and be merry, for tomorrow you die—floating like a feather on the wind.

Jesus took responsibility for the sin of the world and changed history. He took the oldest recorded genealogy and historical document of the Tanakh and used it to give a New Covenant to countless peoples. He changed the past. He opened the Tanakh to all people. He also changed the future. His spiritual presence lives on two thousand years later— helping to spread churches, build hospitals, power education, reduce violence, encourage personal responsibility, and end slavery.

Christ is, of course, an extreme example of integrating the subconscious. He did it perfectly, but others did well: the apostle Paul, Martin Luther, and George Washington changed the stories of the past and influenced the future. This is rich meaningfulness. Everything you do, every second, thought, and feeling—it all matters. The detail and accuracy of the story you tell is important, and it is up to you.

Remember: You do not *have* a spirit—you *are* a spirit that just happens to *have* a body. The threat to spiritual being is meaninglessness. Meaninglessness resides in your body's desires for pleasure and ease. Sure, there are days when you must rest, but it is typically not today. Ignore the stories pushed on you that do not add purpose to life.

Opportunities for Being

What opportunities benefit being? This depends on time, place, and circumstance. Like threats, opportunities are outside of your body, mind, heart, and spirit. So what opportunities to being exist today? More directly, what opportunities to your physical being, mental being, emotional being, and spiritual being exist?

Opportunities for Physical Being: In a culture that is increasingly safer, better fed, and physically (scientifically) understood, opportunities abound. To have secure, powered shelter stocked with customized nutrition, fitness products, and comforts means you can increasingly assess and adapt your physical being to a longer, more meaningful life with greater ease. The "Preston curve," which is the empirical relationship between life expectancy and real capita income, shows that higher income leads to longer life, although there are diminishing returns. The more you can live physically secure, the more you can focus on knowledge, relationships, and spirit.

The overabundance of opportunities for physical being in the developed Western world translates to opportunities for a healthier physical being by denying yourself physical comforts.

You choose to eat healthy, which requires denying what is unhealthy but tastes sweeter and richer. You choose not to eat as an act of courage, discipline, and focus, not out of the desperation that results from a bad hunt or harvest. You choose to learn martial skills without the threat of death. You get in touch with your physical fears and weaknesses by climbing a well-scouted mountain. You learn to push and control your physical abilities in new ways—powerblocking, mountain boarding, or wingsuit flying. You hike in the wilderness with the safety of a mobile phone that provides GPS guidance and access to medical advice. You travel the globe without saying goodbye permanently to your family and community.

Travel is fatal to prejudice, bigotry, and narrow-mindedness, and many of our people need it sorely on these accounts. (Mark Twain)

Look for purposeful and meaningful ways to deny opportunities that satiate the physical. Face threats to physical being and grow in a controlled and meaningful way. Extract maximal meaning out of challenge and physical threat. What a time to be alive! Explore, train, get up and go, assess, adapt, overcome, conquer, and grow.

Opportunities for Mental Being: You live in the Information Age. For the first time in recorded history, you have crossed out of a predominately physical world and into an informational world. Adapt to this world and understand what this means. Those who leverage this capitalize massively on opportunities.

The power of Information Age companies like Google, Microsoft, Amazon, and others is unimaginable! As you live longer and fight for physical survival less, you mentally learn and grow more. You can allocate more resources to knowledge over survival—if you avoid the threats of nonsense like movies, news, funny cat videos, Chinese-made gadgets, or universities spewing hipster stupidity.

Today in the First World, you have access to libraries of meaningful information. Online videos teach music, psychology, religion, philosophy, and more. E-books put the greatest wisdom literature known to humanity at your fingertips. The internet provides access to knowledge resources unimaginable to previous generations.

The real challenge is determining where and why to focus. The more choices offered, the harder it is to choose, and people often opt for the easiest option and not the best. Therefore, focus is vital. However, it's hard to maintain, and when you come home from a hard day at work, there are so many options. Read a book, but which one? Research a subject, but what subject? Focus on what knowledge would best benefit the surrounding environment. Use your peaceful home, coffee shop, or library to develop knowledge that adds value to the world. Find your *why* to overcome the friction of the easier, moving-picture, HD options.

How do you balance all available opportunities for mental being development?

Step one: Have a plan. Example: You determine that computer language could be useful to know.

Step two: Choose your focus. Learn one computer language at a time.

Step three: Start with the older resources and work forward. Start with older, basic codes, and work up to more complex, esoteric modern coding. Then invent your own code.

There is a lot you can focus on, and your focus is a unique balance of interests and needs. I focus on four areas—learning something physical, mental, relational, and spiritual. Three to five is enough to keep the mind engaged in growth but not overwhelm it. College typically includes six classes a semester, but your focus in college is learning and mental development, capitalizing on the learning capabilities of that age. Later, family and career get in the mix and take up mental resources. Learning six things at once might not be possible.

Focus on learning that will move your being toward that which optimizes your value-adding ability. This may mean focusing on home or career. If you're newly married, focus on relating and growing into oneness with your spouse. New parents? Study how to raise good kids. After a career change, adjust your knowledge to succeed. Overcome a sedentary life by learning how to adjust nutrition and exercise. Regain connection and meaning by studying religion and how the spirit applies to life. Grow stronger relationships by studying to become more empathetic and a clearer communicator.

If you read a few books on a subject, you inch toward expertise. One book a week equals fifty books a year, excluding a couple weeks off. Over five, ten, or twenty years, this knowledge adds up. Read a thousand books in twenty years, and you become a valuable employee, successful entrepreneur, or expert in your field. You will truly live in the Information Age!

Opportunities for Emotional Being:

Love sought is good, but given unsought is better. (William Shakespeare, *Twelfth Night*)

How meaningful can you make relationships? Parents glimpse this with children. Fifty-year anniversary-holders know about this. You get an unpleasant taste of it when a good friend betrays you.

If you can learn to be secure in body and mind, then you can build better relationships. Relationships require connection between two people. You must make yourself available and strengthen yourself emotionally. Do not allow relationships that are easy-come, easy-go fool you. Such relationships are superficial because of insecurities on both sides. Think: Can you disagree with the boss's decision? Can you point out fraud in the office?

If your physical world, home, finances, and life are not stable, can you risk your job or career? If you are wealthy, do you suspect relationships exist solely for the money? Do you know enough to critique those around you? Maybe it is better to choose your arguments, but maybe you tell a lie to avoid putting a relationship on the line. Do you challenge the status quo? Are you willing to be disagreeable and risk your heart? This is a confrontational perspective; but the reverse is just as true.

Do you seek criticism from your boss, coworkers, spouse, children, church, town hall, community center, and friends? Probably not. That's why people are afraid to criticize—they cringe when asked. TV stars Simon Cowell (*American Idol*) and Gordon Ramsey (*Hell's Kitchen*) became famous for holding people to a standard. However, people tune in to see them proved wrong, not because they are looking for proper vocal or culinary critiques!

When a spouse, parent, teacher, or boss presents a list of complaints, are you excited to listen? What a missed opportunity! Shunning criticism signals that you have not acted or thought right, currently or in the past. It happens because you are human. Complaints point to mistakes, weaknesses in thought, and action on your part. Your ability to connect relates to your ability to think and act in an integrated way with another person, but seldom are you integrated with yourself. Of course, you will fail at being integrated with others!

Human nature reacts defensively to criticism. Fight this nature and choke down your initial emotional response to criticism. Withhold judgment, look for the uncomfortable truth, and own it. Compare yourself to all you can be; recognize where you are weak, ignorant, and insecure. Acknowledge where you are weak and put your vulnerability—

your heart—on the line; this creates more meaningful connections.

In a modern environment overly concerned about the material and informational, you create power, influence, and value in resisting faux social network, fake outrage, on-demand divorce, single-parent homes, and improper view of employees. In the recent past, survival was barely possible alone. Families were essential. Your ancestors arranged marriages to avoid catastrophe, and you could barely travel beyond your community because it was dangerous to leave those relationships. Laws, codes of conduct, bills of rights, and safer societies have lowered the survival value of relationships.

Jewish people dance for joy at the telling of the law because it makes survival easier. Today, you can survive and live without strong family and community relationships. The number of people living virtual lives is growing fast. Japan calls these individuals *hikikomori*, young shut-ins withdrawn from society. That is why the American baby boomer generation is beset by a hoarding mentality.

The opportunity is obvious: Be good spouses, parents, workers, bosses, and community members. Build meaningful relationships face-to-face, one on one. Rely on other people and encourage them to rely on you. Then forgive those who let you down.

Opportunities for Spiritual Being: There are two opportunities for spiritual development that deserve mention. First, in solitude, focus on that which is greater than you. Second, serve others and let go of your ego.

Your spiritual being grows when you confront suffering and do hard things for others—when you let go of ego and rely on another, forgive a wrong, or learn or do something hard and new. You grow your spiritual being when you disconnect and spend time in solitude contemplating natural law, the divine, and your relationship to the spiritual. Be humbled and commit to that which is greater.

This is hard to do in a concrete world where connection to phones, computers, and social media is ubiquitous. Most leadership misleads, and many of the wealthy and powerful are empty. What is going on here?

As you have read, relationships matter. Your relationship to the divine matters most. You must have quiet time and retreat into solitude. Develop habits of walking alone quietly, spending time in nature, or having a morning devotional time. In the Hebrew Bible, taking time to consecrate or separate yourself for God is a Nazarite vow that can benefit your spiritual being.

Serving others in humility helps you develop spiritually. When you serve out of love and an understanding that you are here for others and the divine, your spirit will be stretched to new heights.

Chapter 12

RELATIONSHIP TO THE WORLD

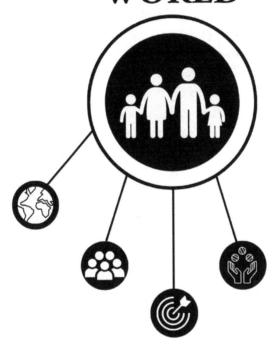

It's not what you look at that matters; it's what you see.
—Henry David Thoreau

The art of war teaches us to rely not on the likelihood of the enemy's not coming, but on our own readiness to receive him; not on the chance of his not attacking, but rather on the fact that we have made our position unassailable.
—Sun Tzu

Perception

As outlined in the previous chapter, your environment is largely outside of your control. Therefore, your perception of the world outside matters. How the world perceives you matters too. Of course, you have less control over the world's perception of you than your perception of the world.

Your perception dictates how you operate and what your priorities are. Perceive the world differently than it is, and frustration ensues. The more accurately you perceive the world, the better your decisions can be.

Likewise, it matters how people perceive you. What do they see: a good, bad, or inconsequential person? How others perceive you may be unfair, but it does not justify lies and manipulation. Also, others' perceptions of you should not affect your self-worth. All you can control are your actions, not people's perceptions. This may require you to act with discretion, but never with deceit.

There are odd dichotomies regarding this. Others should know you care without you saying it. Show them. They may want to hear that you care, but action matters the most. Sometimes when a person is in need, actions and words carry less value. Typically, people do not want help because of their need. They want help because you love or care for them. This is the old aphorism that people do not want a handout but a hand up. Ultimately, what matters in relationships is the outside party's perception: the timing, their preferences, and what you are offering.

This chapter builds on previous chapters—assessing and adapting to your environment. This is the first step toward understanding your world. Next is understanding how you position yourself in the world. In business, such positioning is through a value proposition. This states the unique value a business offers within the industry. For example, a fast-food restaurant has a differing value proposition than a five-star restaurant. This may feel uncouth within individual relationships, but it is true.

A parent has a different relationship than a teacher. If a teacher or adult friend usurps the parent role, there are problems. Spousal relationships are the same. Another person usurps the role of a spouse, and the consequences of such betrayal are severe. The value of the relationship dictates how uniquely you must position. The unique position of father, mother, or spouse is critical, while a friend is less unique and an acquaintance even less so.

Assess your environment accurately to position in ways that add value to others. It's true in dating, job interviewing, going out, or making friends. However, it is an ongoing truth. You are always dating (healthy marriages demand it), always job interviewing (even in the same job), and always trying to be a good parent, friend, or community member. Your relationship to the world is ever-changing, because you are changing, as are others and the world.

Relationships take effort. This is why people grow apart and relationships end prematurely. How can people grow apart when an old friend you have not seen in years can come back into your life and things return as if they never left? The past effort you put into the relationship leads to similar effort in the future when the opportunity presents itself.

It is a choice. People are quick to look for the next thing. They change jobs for more pay and seek a nicer husband, a younger wife, or better friends. It's easier than looking in the mirror and seeing an opportunity for growth. Therefore, they change their environment instead of themselves.

In chapter 9, I wrote about seeking to understand others and listening. The environmental component of relationships involves being there for the people in your life—knowing and hearing them. It is like a service you provide to others, what you were created to do. If you understand what others want, you can make yourself available to them. You can be a good listener, but if your spouse, children, coworkers, friends, and others do not talk to you, you are not helpful. Likewise, you can be in a great place to be a listener without listening and understanding people. In business, marketing and value propositions go together. In relationships, listening and understanding positions you in valuable ways.

Understanding people's perceptions allows you to navigate into helpful positions. You will not always understand others. Complex issues and others' needs make understanding more difficult. After all, you cannot walk in every person's shoes.

The most valuable feedback is usually negative. Negative feedback requires work, which means challenge and position change for you. As you assess and adapt to others' needs, they will better perceive your position, confide in you, and build relationship with you. They will allow you deeper levels of positioning in their minds and hearts.

Perception is a function of position. You can be in the correct position, but others may not perceive it. This is their fault. Or you can be in the correct position but not communicate it, which is your fault. You perceive you are in the correct position, but are incorrectly positioned. Unfortunately, it is typically the latter. People want friends, to be understood, and to be valuable to others. If you are perceived negatively, it is likely because of incorrect position.

When perceived negatively, do you question your perception or change your position? Are you sending mixed signals? Have you positioned yourself to be tired, stressed, unfocused, and undisciplined because you perceive another person wants something different from what you give? Maybe you have positioned yourself in a way the environment does not want; if so, you have failed to assess the needs of your environment properly. The environment could value things you cannot offer, such as feel-good emptiness and imaginary fantasies.

Focus on value. To position in a valuable way that is not manipulative, you must live purposefully with the skills to execute your purpose, knowing yourself while being cognizant of important relationships and leveraging your resources. While you will not perfectly align all five principles, the degree to which you do will dictate the value you provide. "Perfection is the enemy of good." You can apply this truism to relationships with the divine and spouse, along with life as a parent, student, teacher, coworker, leader, or citizen. Based on your perception of purpose, skills, people, environment, and resources, how can you position yourself to bring value? As you navigate in this direction, the territory opens.

Position

Positioning takes work. As mentioned previously, you can manipulate perception. Don't! Perception should aid positioning for the creation of real—not perceived—value. Care how others perceive you and work hard to position in a truly valuable way.

Position is where you are, regardless of perception. Position is physical, mental, emotional, and spiritual. The more aligned your position across all paradigms of being, the higher value your position. You know this intrinsically. A spouse can physically be present, but if not engaging mentally and emotionally, the other spouse may feel unheard.

Aim to position across the spectrum of being to add value. This has different meanings depending on what the relationships value and specific opportunities and threats toward that relationship. A simple way to conceptualize this is through employment.

Some bosses do not care about employees being on the clock at 8 a.m. as long as the work gets done. Other bosses may not value work getting done as long as a seat is filled. Completing your work from 8 a.m. to 4 p.m. or 4 p.m. to midnight may not matter. Some work may require detachment from certain aspects of the work. Therapists who fully empathize with every patient may burn out, and battlefield medics who take every death personally may become ineffective.

Physical Position: Time, geography, and physical ability are examples of how you can position physically. Some things are in your control. Often you can control being on time. Others are not in your control, such as the geographic place where you find yourself. It is hard to be there for someone on the other side of the globe. However, if you are down the street and never show up, it may be worse.

If your job requires you to lift heavy objects every day and you cannot, you will be fired. If you are sick, tired, or in other physically negative states of being, it is hard to be positioned for a meaningful relationship with the world.

In the past, physical positioning was a major component because of limits put on travel, communication, and survival. Today these positioning aspects are more fluid and malleable. However, there remains great opportunity to serve others by being healthy, energetic, and physically available.

Mental Position: You flow between knowledge and an ability to receive new knowledge. The former can hamper the latter if you assent to things that limit your learning. Position your mind in a way that is open to learning and studying new things of importance in your environment as you map out unknown territory. This is important because the world is as informational as it is physical.

Ideally, societal institutions built over hundreds of years provide frames of reference for what is useful and grant early warning of opportunities or threats to being. If you forget the lessons of the past, you are doomed to repeat them.

On the flip side, knowledge can also blind you to new information, because it soothes. Knowledge, which represents the ordered world, is comfortable. The unknown, the world of chaos, is stressful and unpleasant; it requires challenge, risk, and growth. This is how an adult brain learns. The uncomfortable brain signal of error must drown out comfort so that when you learn something new, you recognize it as correct. Surround yourself with feeling good, and you become incapable of recognizing and learning new knowledge. The error signal cannot be detected to embed the new knowledge. Philosophers and sages have always known what science only recently proved.

The impediment to action advances action. What stands in the way becomes the way. (Marcus Aurelius)

Humankind spent a few thousand years learning to survive by building systems, institutions, and knowledge. From Socrates to the Magna Carta and the Torah to the liberties outlined in the US Bill of Rights, people only recently established knowledge enabling humans to die of old age with greater luxury and freedom of expression than ever before. Though wisdom of the past enables you to survive, if you are closed to new knowledge, you will miss out on new threats and opportunities.

This is played out when companies get left behind because their products and services becoming antiquated. It occurs in individual lives too: employees get surprised at being fired and spouses are shocked when served divorce papers.

This is natural; it is how to survive. You make assumptions and turn on autopilot. In this way, life is manageable. If you had to reanalyze everything, you would get nowhere and do nothing. Therefore, you must be careful of mental biases and blind spots. What things do you assume are correct that you should question?

Of course, everything does not deserve scrutiny. Relying on social institutions that teach you to tie your shoes, fundamental math skills, and the rule of law leads to ordered society. You can develop a stronger mental map of your position in the world by withholding judgment on things of which you are uncertain.

Your mental positioning must be developed within the context of your family, work, and community. President John Adams recognized his place in time and history. He recognized his natural abilities, the needs of those around him, and the needs of his greater community.

> I must study politics and war, that our sons may have liberty to study mathematics and philosophy. Our sons ought to study mathematics and philosophy, geography, natural history and naval architecture, navigation, commerce and agriculture in order to give their children a right to study painting, poetry, music, architecture, statuary, tapestry and porcelain. (John Adams)

Art, music, entertainment, and other creative endeavors provide great value. However, the world around you may need something else. Be aware of your relationship to the world to identify and meet these needs.

Emotional Position: Try building your emotional position relative to your physical and mental positions. The world and others need you in times and places of challenge, difficulty, and discomfort. If you place yourself in challenging physical and mental spaces but cannot exist there emotionally, others may not perceive you as holding those physical and mental positions.

Is the position truly physically and mentally challenging? Is it filled with failure, pain, and growth if it fosters no emotional response? When positioned in meaningful ways, these positions trigger desires, hopes, and dreams.

If you give in to emotional reactions when confronted with mental and physical pain (that is, you tune out the emotions), then your ability to get meaning from these places will decrease. For this reason, emotional position relies on two critical actions. First, you must feel the position's emotion without reacting to it. Only sociopaths or the mentally ill cannot feel sadness, fear, or pain. These are acceptable emotional spaces. As you move out of territory you understand into places of chaos and dysfunction where you can serve, it is natural to feel negative emotions. Learn to stoically accept these realities for what they are and what they say about you, your weaknesses, and your frailty.

Second, once you accept the challenge of the position, be honest about the emotional challenges the position presents. Bury and repress the painful state in which you exist, and you are being manipulative. This false bravado can be hard to let go. Honesty in challenging emotional places allows you to deal with the pain of the situation correctly. If you are dishonest about the uncomfortable position, you may take expedient ways to resolve the uncomfortable position that are not beneficial and will impact all affected parties' understanding of the reason behind the resolution.

Feeling and honesty enable you to deal with emotionally challenging situations. Dealing with angry or upset people is difficult. The natural reaction to such people is fight or flight, but neither is helpful when dealing with emotionally charged people. You must feel the emotions of the position, recognize the person is angry, and avoid reacting. This can be difficult if you misread emotions. Grief goes through emotional phases that manifest as denial, anger, depression, release, and hopefully a return to love. By allowing a person to experience feelings without reaction, you let them vent. This allows for a fuller expression of the situation and can defuse the situation.

Additionally, you should recognize the person's emotions, admit this makes you feel uncomfortable, and work to resolve the issue. Use calm, nonreactive questioning to gain a truer understanding of the person and/ or situation. In a worst-case scenario, when you cannot handle a situation in a nonreactive way, move directly to this step, admitting you cannot deal with this emotional situation. Express your need for space, time, or help, and reposition yourself to be helpful. If you cannot handle face-to-face confrontation, have the issue outlined in written form; or if you cannot deal with it today, follow up on a later date.

Uncontrolled emotional reactions often come from particularly sensitive areas, such as family or money, or during times of weakness—when you're tired or stressed. When a person controls emotions in sensitive areas during times of weakness, this is true mastery. My father is an example of this, as are William Wilberforce and Abraham Lincoln. Each managed great emotional conflict without allowing it to control and manipulate their lives.

Spiritual Position: Spiritual positioning is difficult to conceptualize. Yet it exists. People can position themselves in powerfully spiritual places.

> Our struggle is not against flesh and blood, but against the rulers, against the powers, against the world forces of this darkness, and against the spiritual forces of wickedness in the heavenly places. (Ephesians 6:12 NASB)

Spiritual positioning is akin to spiritual warfare. Chaos, evil, the devil—however you define it, can be insidious. All things spiral toward chaos, nature takes back what is hers, cities crumble into ruin, and in a few generations humanity forgets; and if you do not actively pursue what is orderly and virtuous, your life can spiral into victimhood and unnecessary suffering.

The spiritual environment can be deceiving, which you know from a character most religious texts name "deceiver." Imagination can tempt you in ways contrary to nature, virtue, and good. You feel accused, causing you to cower in shame and inaction.

When you are deceived, your actions are erroneous. You could live a faux spiritual life following empty promises and foolish wisdom. You could be deceived into believing you are good—that you stand on the side of justice and what is right. People deceived in this way set themselves up as tyrants over themselves and others! You can be tempted and press forward into unhealthy action, convinced the action is healthy and good by justifying the temptation's benefit. Accused, you can fill with shame and brokenness, which stops you in your tracks and keeps you from maneuvering or positioning yourself in search of light and truth.

How do you avoid the spiritual dangers of deception, temptation, and accusation? By seeking the truth. You will never have all truth, but you can know some. Truth protects you from wrong action and reveals existing areas of weakness outside the territory that it occupies. If you know something as truth, that truth may apply to other areas.

How do you know what truth is? There are several rules of thumb. Ask yourself these questions: What has lasted the test of time (the Lindy effect)? What is in alignment with the natural laws of the world? What is useful for the renewing of your mind?

Deception often accompanies temptation, but not always. Moderation may not be intrinsically bad. Everyone needs a day off, an ice cream scoop, or some mindless entertainment. Giving in to temptation happens when they become life. You live for the weekend, the next good meal, or the next episode. A little ice cream cannot hurt and surfing social media does not end the world, but these are dopamine-generating substances with no real value. Build a citadel around your heart! Do not allow emotions, reason, and the material to blind you to the spiritual danger around you.

You are susceptible to not seeing the truth and risking weakness in the face of temptation. Therefore, the hardest place to position yourself spiritually is where you are free from the accusations and guilt of your past. You cannot save yourself from your past mistakes. You exist in time, and what you did is now part of history. Every second of your life, along with your ancestors' choices and your parents' mistakes, has contributed to your life's missteps, lost focus, failed discipline, and meaninglessness.

This should lead you to value moments in time. Get up and do not succumb to guilt. Search for that which redeems things out of time! Harness your conviction to fuel your search for truth. Deal with guilt by continuing the search for truth and use it to overcome temptation. The Spirit has all the answers and strength you need.

Troubleshooting

Others' perception of you is their reality. It determines their behavior toward you. Because of this, all the elements of positioning—physical, mental, emotional, and spiritual—create a perception of you. Everything you do matters—big and small.

Put in the effort to know and understand others' perception, then you must contrast this with how you are perceived. The difference between the two represents a gap you must navigate. This is a constant and ongoing series of maneuvering into better positions.

You likely are comfortable in your current position, even if you know it is not ideal: a routine job with limited growth potential, a stagnant relationship, a daily routine that impacts your health, and a spiritual life leading nowhere. Moving into a new position will probably be challenging and full of disruption. For this reason, "cover your bases"—a military phrase for setting up defensive positioning. When you cover your bases, you assess the environmental risks to your secured and ordered position. It requires you to think through your weaknesses and determine how to shore up those weaknesses.

If your life is stable and orderly, it can be a place where you can return. For example, you can take on a side hustle in your free time without sacrificing paid employment. This has risk if your job is in a precarious position. A loss of focus could cause you to get fired—thus, to cover your bases, you must maintain focus at work. However, it is helpful to know when a base is not worth covering. Getting an outside perspective is a great way to cover your bases. Friends, family members, spiritual leaders, mentors, and therapists are potential sources for improving perspective.

Flow is a state of existence between high levels of challenge and high levels of skill. As you position in the world along the four states of being, you will do it imperfectly. To the extent you can adjust position, you can improve it. Typically, where you experience low-level challenge, you are bored, relaxed, and perhaps comforted. If you could do more, you may feel conviction or anxiety to do so. However, as the challenge of your position changes into harder and more meaningful endeavors, worry, heightened anxiety, and fear can arise.

While testing the balance between skill and challenge, the natural tendency is to pull back. You fear loss of control. As you push into overly challenging areas of position, fear and panic show up because your skill level does not match. This can be healthy. When placing yourself in dangerous places where you do not have the skill to exist, fear is appropriate. Just remember that you learn and grow skills only in challenge. As you learn the balance between control and panic, you learn to exist in new positions.

If you are constantly anxious and panicky, you pushed too far. Pull back, reassess, and regain control. When you are constantly in a mode of relaxed control, boredom, and apathy, you are not walking the right path. Seek balance between these states: flow.

Flow is where you chart new positions, uncover new meaning, and develop new skill. Use flow for troubleshooting, but not as an absolute. Video games, surfing, martial arts, and other activities where you can find flow are not intrinsically good. Video games are designed for instant flow that scales to the big boss fight at the end, keeping you hooked for hours of flow play. But is that flow state creating something meaningful in a physical, mental, emotional, or spiritual sense?

Chapter 13

THE BROADER WORLD

If you don't have a competitive advantage, don't compete.

—Jack Welch

Wonderful castles, surrounded by deep, dangerous moats where the leader inside is an honest and decent person. Preferably, the castle gets its strength from the genius inside; the moat is permanent and acts as a powerful deterrent to those considering an attack; and inside, the leader makes gold but doesn't keep it all for himself. Roughly translated, we like great companies with dominant positions, whose franchise is hard to duplicate and has tremendous staying power or some permanence to it.

—Warren Buffett

Competitive Landscape

As you think about the world and your place in it, you may be tempted to take a positive or negative perspective. Positively, you can move and exist within this world. In the developed Western world, you have a certain amount of wealth and freedom. Negatively, you are not in control of the world, and you know little. Your skills, relationships, and meaning are not enough to garner the control you desire.

It can be tempting to view the world as a pacified place. However, other actors—people or nature—may not have your best interest in mind. The world may act contrary to your desires randomly or with intention. Others may shift suffering from themselves and onto you. They may truly wish you harm. In Western comfort, this is easy to forget.

Competition increases relational complexity. It increases the desire to understand the world's motives. How can you compete with or avoid that which brings no meaning into your life? After all, the person or organization that does not survive ceases to benefit the world.

Competition builds skills, strengthens relationships, tests the resolve of purpose, and helps uncover untapped resources. The more communities and organizations operate competitively, the greater meaning, skills, relationships, and resources society enjoys. Humanity must learn and coexist together and competitively. There are incompatible ideologies and beliefs, but you can overcome these ideologies—whether physical, mental, emotional, or spiritual. If you cannot, you must adapt and grow to survive—or learn to abandon the meaningless.

Competition is not always intentional. You compete with nature for survival, but nature is indifferent to your survival. You must look for ways to still be uniquely effective. In everyday life, this may not be intentional. Your point of uniqueness is where you can compete.

In war, these are called "force multipliers"—surprise, organization, morale, mobility, technology, reputation, weather, training, and intelligence. In business, they are "competitive advantages." They involve the differentiation of a product or service focused on a certain market. Example: tools are designed for the craftsman, novice, or laborer.

The most known point of differentiation is cost. However, cost is the weakest point of differentiation. Someone can almost always make a cheaper, weaker, poorer product. In broader communities, these competitive advantages could be benefits. Geographic communities benefit from location, political structure, or business environment. Religious communities have benefits extending from their doctrine or creed. For the individual, this is what makes you unique.

A community seeking to survive and compete for dollars, people, or victory must have a point of positive differentiation. The best type adds value. It offers higher quality, more functionality, greater meaning, better design, first or more timely delivery, better location, more personalized, or more integrative. For organizations or communities, finding this positive differentiation is a critical step toward success. This applies to individuals too. You want to be unique, loved, and cared for as special. The beautiful thing is that you are unique and special; sometimes it is just hard to see.

The more unique, valuable, and positive the differentiation, the better a community can compete. To identify differentiation, you must know the product, service, community, or organization inside and out. How would you sell a digital recording system for brain-scanning neurological research? You must know how they are different. The salesperson selling these devices knows. I do not! The deeper your knowledge, the more you will know what makes it special or how it could become specialized.

Additionally, you must know your competitors. This helps you know what is different about your item. The positive differentiation is where you offer value. However, positive differentiation does not guarantee success—you must fill a pain point, as discussed in chapter 10. A need must be met within the market.

Another way to analyze the competitive landscape is through the lens of opportunities and threats. Understanding the environment in a detailed manner can show how competition will evolve and challenges it may bring. Organizational areas to analyze include trends in technology, economics, demographics, geography, environment, law, politics, and culture. Try a PESTEL analysis. Changes in these areas represent potential opportunities and threats. Analyze how they will affect your community or market, needed and unneeded skills, resources, and your competition.

Of course, cultural changes affect individuals too, but large demographic, political, legal, and cultural shifts are dealt with at organizational and community levels. Individuals seldom have much control over large cultural changes outside of their communities. As the complexity of community increases, it becomes harder for individuals to influence or control outcomes.

While leading a community was once like riding a horse, it may become like riding a tiger. This does not negate the need for communities to take care when affecting individual lives. When community leadership missteps, individuals down the chain will suffer. Principles by which a community exists or an individual lives determines the community's ability to self-regulate and the individual's ability to rise above a failing community.

Leadership must assess the competitive landscape of the environment and take responsibility for adapting to it. It is hard at an individual level to hold sway over an entire community. Beware individuals seeking to do this.

Economic Moats and Value Propositions

You can leverage strategic advantages in several ways. Invent something new, and patents and trademarks can solidify and protect your position to an extent. *New* is hard, and nothing stays new for long. If you move into the market first or have special connections to those you serve, you can build relationships that provide protection from competition. Provide higher-quality services, products, or ideas, and you enjoy a particular advantage.

An individual, organization, or community skill set allows you to better navigate the competitive landscape. Where you provide a positively differentiated product, service, or idea, build on and enhance the desired differentiation to better position within the landscape. Where you have a lower cost or higher level of productivity, you can undercut the competition.

These five items—patents/trademarks, customer relationships, capabilities, differentiation, and cost—are known as economic moats

(Porter 1985). Although helpful tools, they vary in strength and do not guarantee success. You can work around a patent, disrupt relationships, develop your own capabilities, further differentiate, and produce a cheaper product.

In the business world, competition is fierce. Failure to have an economic moat leads to ruin. Competition for larger communities— cities or nations, for example—is also steep, but gets played out over longer periods at nearly imperceptible levels until reaching a tipping point.

The best moat is capabilities. A person, business, or community can always develop unique and valuable skills. Unique skills and abilities stand out in a competitive landscape. This is what makes sporting events fun to watch. Of course, capabilities equate to hard work and many shy from this. People want a 100-percent unique, patented product they can sell and walk off in peace and prosperity. Nothing valuable comes without developing a skill that is valued by the broader world. The harder a skill is to develop, the better the product, service, or idea that proceeds from it.

Once you develop a competitive advantage, you must communicate and visualize how to leverage it. A value proposition is a statement of the value provided. It allows you to position your community, organization, or self within the minds of those you serve in relationship to the other voices begging for attention, dollars, time, or effort of your audience. It applies to schoolteachers, parents, spouses, churches, towns, businesses, employees, and everyone in between.

A value proposition answers four critical questions: What is the purpose or impact of the thing being proposed? Does this product, service, organization, community, or individual have the skills to deliver this impact? Do they have proof of the claims of impact and skill to deliver? What is the cost (physical, mental, emotional, or spiritual) to receive this thing?

The value proposition of this book is as follows: *Five Principles* provides a process for living a meaningful and fruitful life. It integrates five foundational principles to guide you in the development of the skills, relationships, and resources that help you to position yourself effectively within your environment to discover maximum meaning in life. Throughout history, businesses, communities, and individuals of all types have achieved lasting and meaningful success using these principles. This book is an affordable guide to these principles and an easy read to help you along this path. The true price is in the purposeful, focused, and disciplined execution of the principles in this book.

Impact is the promise. This book's impact is living a meaningful, fruitful life. To the extent this book achieves its purpose, I will have leveraged my skills of integrating meaningful principles, communicating, differentiating the book from other content, and investing resources into the book's conceptualization and distribution. As noted, this book contains five principles that provide a foundation for a meaningful and fruitful life. Proof and cost follow: the book will be affordable. However, the true price is what you invest into the individual execution of these principles.

A consulting firm may promise improved revenue. It outlines the skills of its consultants, provides evidence of past success, and offers a free analysis to better understand the potential client.

Parents may promise to equip a child for adulthood. They outline their abilities of being an adult and the path to adulthood, and they come to an agreement with the child on what this will look like for the cost.

A value proposition can be for anything: a product, service, or idea. A business should have a value proposition for each product line or service it offers. A value proposition can be short or long, but it should always be clear, meaningful, and to the point.

Dangerous World

Communities, organizations, and individuals compete. Americans once understood this—the grand experiment, the upstart nation, unleashed on the world of free competition.

During my freshman year of college, there was a guy in one of my classes who studied all the time! At eighteen, this guy was absolutely getting after it. I asked why. He said he grew up in Sarajevo and came straight to college out of a war-torn city. The siege of Sarajevo ended in February 1996, eighteen months before our semester began. The siege was the longest on a capital city in modern history. This student grew up surrounded by the sounds of mortar shell explosions. He had no intention of going back. The immigrant and stranger is a threat, but he is an even greater opportunity!

It is a blessing to be exposed to different cultures and peoples. The above story is common in a nation of immigrants. My family entered through Jamestown; my ancestors carved a niche in the mountains with hard work and bloodshed. Why do people not return to third-world countries? Persecution. No opportunities. Wrong political parties. Why do the favelas of Brazil produce dominance in soccer and martial arts? It is a rare individual who trades prosperity for slums.

For political reasons, my graduate school roommate from China was not allowed into the Communist Party, so he came to the United States, earned two master's degrees, and then passed the CPA exam! I have met no one with greater work ethic, and I know many hardworking people.

The developed Western world takes much freedom and opportunity for granted with shameful complacency and laziness. The path to physical, mental, emotional, and spiritual weakness is being laid before Western civilization. We do not have an excuse, but we make them—inner city, Rust Belt, country redneck, no opportunities, racial minority, and other nonsense. Freedom is opportunity!

Not everyone has the best motives. Many are driven by greed, envy, lust, and hate. These are your coworkers, CEOs, community leaders, and national leaders. Just because you prefer empathy, expressiveness, or analysis does not mean you cannot have your lunch taken, business put into bankruptcy, or community overrun by those who seek chaos.

On top of this, most people do not have meaningful motives in their life. They are driven by a desire for the easy road. They think heaven is a place in the clouds for those who say magic words. For now, they just want to eat, drink, and be merry. Holy Scripture has harsh words (Rev. 3:16) for lukewarm people walking a fruitless path. Meaninglessness creates a dangerous world. What is expedient is seldom good. It is the fool led by the one sowing chaos who is hard to handle. Why? Because it is hard to tell the difference between the fool and the devil. The fool deserves compassion while the devil hell.

Because the world is a dangerous place, you cannot ignore the competitive landscape of the world. If it does not physically kill you, it will drain you mentally, hurt you emotionally, and leave a spiritual void. This happens in brief moments when you let down your guard and turn from the path. In the broader world, your principles must guide your decisions and see you through dark times. You must sow correct policies into your communities that focus on what is meaningful over what is expedient or chaotic.

PART V
RESOURCES

Chapter 14

YOUR RESOURCES

Set your minds on things above, not on earthly things.
—Colossians 3:2 (NIV)

Time management is an oxymoron. Time is beyond our control, and the clock keeps ticking regardless of how we lead our lives. Priority management is the answer to maximizing the time we have.
—John C. Maxwell

Resources

Resources are anything used to accomplish a task: lumber to build a house, money to buy the lumber, time to make the money and build the house. Knowledge helps you know how to build a house. People erect the frame. Your environment supplies air to breathe and water to drink. Your abilities and skills are resources that increase and decrease based on their use. In fact, you have more resources at your disposal than you will ever need. Most struggle to know where to start.

In modern times, primary resources are becoming less tangible. Money is a common resource with no intrinsic value. It is completely intangible but powerful, because it is easy to quantify! You can count it, save it, invest it, spend it, and waste it. Knowledge is another powerful intangible resource. In today's world, it is the most powerful resource. Resources of emotion and spirit exist too. Emotional intelligence and spiritual gifts are hard to conceptualize, but they are vital. As humanity grows and finds physical and mental limits, it can grow in emotional maturity and spiritual enlightenment. This leads to your most important resource individual time.

Time

Never seem to find the time
Plans that either come to naught
Or half a page of scribbled lines
("Time" by Pink Floyd)

Time is the most important resource, yet knowledge is the most powerful. However, knowledge is powerful only when used. The use or execution of knowledge is skill.

Time is a finite resource that is absolute equality. Every person has the same number of hours, minutes, and seconds in a day. No one, not even the most powerful people in the world, can save time. All spend time second by second. No one controls how many seconds, minutes, hours, or days they get.

You exist in time. If future humans live hundreds, thousands, or millions of years, they will still exist within the confines of time. However, theoretically, around 10 to the 32,000th years in the future—after the universe stretches so far that not even light can travel the distances, all black holes have evaporated, and the final supernovas wink out, leaving a silent, frozen void of a universe—time will no longer have meaning (Delbert 2020). But humanity will be long gone by then.

Because time is finite, it is immeasurably valuable. So fight against the clock! Consider how you spend your moments. Life management is time management. Though you cannot control time, you can control your focus. To extract the meaning and benefit from any moment, focus on your priorities.

Better use of time leads to better overall resource management. If you spend time in a disciplined manner, you will use your hours in effective ways, gathering other resources such as money, material things, relationships, and knowledge. Waste time and you will fail at gathering needed resources. The challenge is threefold: managing purpose, focus, and discipline.

Most people do not know how to spend time. Without purpose, you spend time on the inexpedient—watching TV, playing games, and goofing off. Everyone needs to relax, goof off, chill out, and live in the moment. The problem is that when you are purposeless, you default toward what is easiest, not toward what is needed. This leads to addictions.

Another issue with resource utilization is focus. You may know what your purpose is. You may be an exemplary employee, outstanding husband, or invested community member, but what should your focus be? If purpose is what you should do, focus is how you should do it.

The final issue of resource utilization is discipline. Often you know what and how to do a thing, yet you do not do it. For maximum resource utilization, you must get all three aligned. Typically, stronger purpose and focus make discipline come easier. Hence why students cram for tests, employees make hard deadlines, and animals fight for survival. Stress and pain can motivate discipline, but the reverse is true as well. Discipline lends greater control over purpose and more flexibility with focus.

Purpose

This book is largely focused on purpose. In chapter 1, purpose is found in confronting suffering. Doing what is hard and meaningful across the four paradigms of being lessens suffering. Chapter 17 revisits purpose with greater detail and gives more guidance on developing your life purpose. If you can articulate your life purpose, you are positioned to manage your life and resources. When your purpose is clear and concise, you know the value of your time and can make wise choices regarding it.

Discipline

Everything discussed in this book takes discipline. Living purposefully, developing skills, building relationships, navigating treacherous environments, and effectively using resources are all highly disciplined modes of being. It does not take discipline to live a meaningless, ignorant, selfish, poorly navigated life. So how do you develop discipline? Where does it come from?

As a child, you received discipline from your parents. Good parents instill discipline in their children. As an employee, your boss instills discipline (called *motivation*), as do teachers and leaders in various hierarchies of competence. However, for your personal, individualized purpose, discipline must come from within. The leadership, ownership, and discipline guru Jocko Willink has this to say about the origins of self-discipline:

> It comes when you make a decision to be disciplined. When you make a decision to be better. When you make a decision to do more, to *be* more. Self-discipline comes when you decide to make a mark on the world. So where does it come from? It comes from you. (*Discipline Equals Freedom: Field Manual* [6–7], St. Martin's Press, Kindle edition)

Can someone without discipline learn discipline? *Discipline* covers drive, motivation, that internal feeling that you are meant for something, calling, and destiny. Every person has a spark of it inside them. Most people beat the spark down into nothing, and some completely extinguish it. In a world of growing physical and informational mastery, discipline of the body and mind are obtainable. Many satiate that motivating spirit with physical and mental discipline, never to wage war with their hearts and rid themselves of ego. Since you were disciplined enough to get this far in this book, you have that spark!

Focus

Focus is crucial to life and time management. It requires purpose, because without purpose your focus can divert to the meaningless. Focus requires discipline to concentrate on what is difficult, brings value, and meaningfulness. Specific focus comes from planning. You can have purpose but no plan or focus. You can have Navy SEAL-level discipline while digging a ditch to nowhere. Countless disciplined people are wealthy but depressed, lost after winning the championship, and surrounded by empty relationships.

In simple terms, you should focus with discipline on what is truly purposeful. As Stephen Covey said, "Begin with the end in mind." Knowing your end purpose will help you find focus. Humans have a limited ability to focus. That is why you cannot read a book while playing the piano and carrying on a conversation at the same time. Focus demands a single object. It is okay to have multiple purposes—to strive to be an excellent employee, husband, father, and community member. Those ideals can be your purpose, but focus becomes strained when you add talented chef, star musician, award-winning writer, basketball MVP, historian, naturalist, entrepreneur, and religious acolyte. Add the constraints of limited time, and it is nearly impossible to focus.

Focused purpose implies picking what is most meaningful, which is typically between three and five things. This limits your focus without fixating on one thing. By having a few disciplined goals, you can incorporate different aspects of your being into your focused purpose. You can use rest and space; you can step away from one area and gain perspective. Ideally, focus is balanced, although life seasons may find you focusing on few items or broadening your perspective. Focus on purpose by weighing a few "big audacious goals" (Collins 2001). This is the start of focused resource use.

What is your purpose in life? Your purpose may be to bring glory to God, be part of a family or community, serve others, and care for your own being. As you develop a plan for a meaningful life, focus becomes more important.

Where is your attention? Big goals are important, but big is also scary and challenging. How do you eat an elephant? One bite at a time. You must break down big, scary goals into smaller pieces—individual objectives that lead toward the bigger goal. By focusing on smaller pieces, you move toward your purpose and a meaningful life.

Five Principles is designed to serve as a guide for focus. Each section helps with individual development of objectives for serving purpose, the overall goal. Part I jump-starts things by talking about meaning. Next is the need for skill to serve that purpose. Learn, practice, sharpen your skill set, and seek teachers and partners to accomplish these goals. Skills lead you to part III, including relationships, communication, listening to others, and being honest with yourself so you can be honest with others. You learn the necessity of risking your heart and building relationships that make you better because you risked and experienced pain and hurt. It means navigating the environment of relationships to position yourself to be competitive by providing something of value. Finally, you arrive at resources, where you must pick a focus that will effectively build skills, develop relationships, and position you in service of that which is meaningful. *Five Principles* outlines how to plan out the focus for any goal: have a purpose, develop skill, build relationships, navigate the environment to provide value, and effectively leverage resources.

If living a meaningful life is the goal, then the other principles—skill, people, environment, and resources—are individual objectives that lead to actualizing that meaning. If you want to do something meaningful, you need the skills, people, environment, and resources to do it.

This is where planning becomes critically important. Planning must take place outside of your head. Carve them into stone, write them on paper, or tap them into a computer—but make them tangible. The more disciplined your planning, the better your focus. In a detailed plan, you see each successive bite of the elephant, which are easier to execute and generate more discipline. It feels good to accomplish a goal, and your brain loves achieving mini-goals. Success begets success.

As you analyze your strengths and weaknesses, who you serve, what those you serve want, where you can position for value, and your resources, the gaps between the ideal need and the current position become apparent.

Here is a simplified example from a spousal perspective:
• Purpose: Be a good spouse.
• Skills:
    • Strength: good listener
    • Strength: romantic
    • Weakness: short temper
    • Weakness: forgetful
• People: Spouse
    • Desires: to be understood
    • Desires: more help around the house
• Environment: Home
    • Threat: too many hours at the office
    • Opportunity: spend more time with spouse
• Resources: Time and Self
    • Give spouse more time—do not waste time at the office. Get home.
    • Give more of self. Be more engaged at home. Do not forget important things.

This simple analysis could apply to many people. However, if you are married, a primary goal should be to serve your spouse by being a good spouse! If married, create a detailed breakdown of your purpose, weaknesses and strengths you bring to the relationship, your spouse's wants and needs, opportunities and threats to your relationship purpose, and resources that can help you become a good spouse.

This example shows how developing anger-management skills are beneficial. This person could focus on learning about anger management instead of wasting time elsewhere. Forgetfulness should also be addressed. It is likely that forgetfulness is generating other issues. The spouse has probably asked for help from the other spouse, who keeps forgetting. Put a to-do list on the fridge! Finally, too much time at the office does not help. This person should update some office skills to work more quickly. Getting home, helping, listening, and being available go a long way toward a stronger relationship.

Here is the focus, objectives on this personal path to a meaningful marriage:

- Be a good spouse by focusing on three objectives:
- Learning to manage your temper.
- Mitigate forgetfulness by using lists.
- Spending less time at the office and more time at home listening and doing.

These examples are simple. The power comes in revisiting the objectives of becoming more skilled, serving people, navigating the environment, and using resources more wisely. After a set period, revisit the list and ask what has changed, what is working, and what is not working.

Dig into the details. Being a good spouse has infinite depth! Becoming a better lover, building a better home, being the ideal match mentally and emotionally to another human, and carving out meaning together are infinitely detailed goals. Choose three to five meaningful sub-objectives to focus on, as in the list above.

As you become more successful at managing focus, you value smaller increments of time. Try getting an appointment with a doctor or lawyer, and you deal with fifteen- or thirty-minute blocks of time. Schedule with a billionaire or president, and you may get time for a thirty-second pitch if you are fortunate. Before you can value such small increments, you must start on bigger blocks. Larger blocks of time—eight-hour shifts or full days—are a good start.

Imagine if you planned out the day and wasted no time. Every second gets used to move toward becoming a good spouse. Quickly, you become one. Granted, you cannot focus twenty-four hours a day on being a good spouse. You would neglect your other duties and drive your spouse crazy. Split between three to five overarching purposes and three to five sub-objectives per overarching purpose. You will get good at them quickly if you maintain discipline and focus.

Remember these rules of thumb. 1. Plan your time on paper or computer. Write it, type it, calendar it, and/or list it. Take the intangible and make it tangible. 2. Start with the end goal in mind. Describe it as a SMART goal. SMART goals are specific, measurable, achievable, relevant, and timely (B. Tracy 2021). 3. Break down the big-picture goal into smaller objectives to be carried out over years, months, or days. 4. Do annual and semiannual big-picture planning and analysis. 5. Do monthly sub-purpose planning and reviews to maintain focus. At the end of each month or quarter, review and plan for the following month or quarter.

It is important to question yourself during planning reviews. Ask: Where am I behind or ahead of my goal? Are there meaningless tasks and jobs that must get cleared out before getting to the meaningful stuff? As time frames that matter shrink, question them intentionally. Avoid trivial pursuits, emotional avoidance, and time-wasting busy work. Poor discipline and bad positioning lead to meaningless distractions and unplanned problems. Manage the areas of discipline and positioning to avoid constant urgent but meaningless work.

The more meaningful something is, the more time you should invest. Likewise, the more timeless something is, the more value it offers. Not every task is completely meaningful and not everything you do is completely timeless. Less meaningful tasks that are substantially time bound, like a crisis, should be handled efficiently. Time management reviews should focus on investing

Specific—Write out clear, concise goals
Measurable—The ability to track progress
Achievable—Set challenging yet achievable goals
Relevant—Pertains to your overarching purpose
Timely—Goal has a target time attached

increasing amounts of time on timeless, loving, deeply meaningful, creative, spiritual, and valuable tasks.

FIVE PRINCIPLES
TIME MANAGEMENT FOCUS

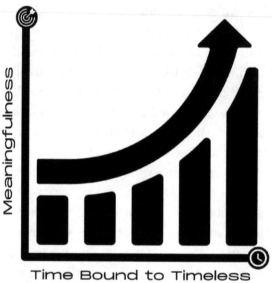

Weekly planning can help you stay the course. You can plan on Friday before leaving the office, first thing Monday morning, or Sunday evening before starting the work week. Review your daily to-do list and calendar at the start of each week, then get after it.

There are great planning methodologies to adapt to your life and circumstances. Brian Tracy's GOSPA (Goals, Objectives, Strategies, Plans, and Actions) method, Stephen Covey's Covey Time Management Matrix, David Allen's "Get Things Done," the infamous PDSA (Plan, Do, Study, Act) method, health care's QAPI (Quality Assurance and Performance Improvement) process, and the military's OODA (Observe, Orient, Decide, Act) Loop are all excellent. If you feel pressed for time, read up on these concepts.

Money

It's a gas
Grab that cash with both hands and make a stash
("Money" by Pink Floyd)

You should always invest a portion of your resources! Albert Einstein said, "Compound interest is the eighth wonder of the world. He who understands it, earns it. He who doesn't—pays it. It is the most powerful force in the universe and the greatest mathematical discovery of all time."

What is compound interest? It is interest earned on interest. Investing $100 at 4 percent earns $4 in the first year. In the second year, it earns 4 percent of $104, which is 16 cents more. It makes even more in future years. Put $100 a month in an investment that mirrors average stock market returns of 8 percent for forty-five working years and you accumulate $463,000, while you contributed only $54,000. Take a 2023 median US household income of $59,000 and invest 10 percent annually at 8 percent, and you will be a multimillionaire by 65.

Financial advisers recommend you save at least 10 percent. If you cannot, start with 1 percent; then increase your giving each month or quarter until you reach 10 percent. Start with a savings account that earns some interest. Once you build a balance, transfer it to an investing account and keep building that nest egg. Need help understanding investing? Hire a financial adviser, read a book, purchase an investing newsletter, recognize you will make mistakes, and learn. Plan prudently, sacrificing today for something of greater future meaning.

With investing, money is not the only area that matters. It is just easier to invest because you can calculate the math and control for risk. You should also invest in your career, relationships, and personal development. Invest in yourself in meaningful, focused, and disciplined ways.

When investing, ask if an investment is good for the paradigms of being: body, heart, mind, and spirit? If the answer is yes, invest. A dead-end job pays the bills, so get the work done and get out. Save your energy to invest in learning, relationships, or doing good in community or church. If a friend always causes trouble, invest elsewhere. If you are alone, lonely, and desperate for a relationship, stop investing in drinks at the bar and invest in building yourself into a healthier, smarter, more stable person who is attractive to others.

The 10-percent rule applies across the spectrum of nonfinancial matters. If you work forty hours a week and sleep fifty-six, you have over seventy hours left. Using the 10 percent rule, you should invest in your body seven hours, mind seven hours, heart seven hours, and spirit seven hours every week. That gives an hour a day for each paradigm of being, leaving forty-four hours a week for travel, hygiene, eating, and goofing off. Guess what—it works! Invest an hour every day into your body, and in a year: transformation. Invest across the four paradigms of being for four hours a day and you will transform your entire life in a year—guaranteed!

Invest in purpose, skills, relationships, adding value in your environment, and being disciplined and focused with resources, your world will change.

Chapter 15

RELATIONSHIP RESOURCES

Ponder for a long time whether you shall admit a given person to your friendship; but when you have decided to admit him, welcome him with all your heart and soul. Speak as boldly with him as with yourself.

—Seneca, "On True and False Friendship"

Walk with the wise and become wise, for a companion of fools suffers harm.

—Proverbs 13:20 (NIV)

The Resource of Relationships

Relationships matter, perhaps now more than ever. As humanity masters the physical world and makes great leaps of knowledge, the new frontier would seem emotional or relational. However, technological leaps meant to connect us in virtual and digital worlds are causing us to discount the importance of relationship!

In the developed world, people no longer borrow sugar from neighbors. Many neighbors barely even talk. If you live in a big city, you may not know your neighbors, and you may have a legitimate fear of them. The traditional tribe is dying, and something else is taking its place.

Relationships as a resource may seem flippant, but they should not be viewed that way! You invest money, fix your home, learn new skills and knowledge, and manage your time. Why not be conscientious in how you handle relationships? Bring purpose, discipline, and focus to your relationships. Consider where and to what purpose you use your time and effort.

Some relationships are toxic. Be careful undertaking a relationship to save another person. A lifeguard requires special training to avoid being drowned by the person they intend to save. Many surround themselves with drowning people because it makes them feel good to help. In the end, they get pulled under.

Lifeguards dive under and swim around the person drowning. The rescuer approaches the drowning victim from behind and grabs the person in a way to restrain them. If the rescuer approaches from the front, the drowning person will grab the lifeguard like a raft and climb onto them. This results in both lives being lost. The person attempting an act of heroism is often in more danger than the person being saved. Police enter the line of fire. Firefighters climb into burning buildings. Doctors, nurses, counselors, and others who guide people walk a fine line between giving a person the tools to improve their own well-being and becoming caught up in the emotional challenges of poor health, death, or emotional, physical, and spiritual suffering.

Do not take me wrong. There may come a time when a close

relationship needs saving. Drug addiction, health problems, and other crises arise with friends, extended family members, spouses, and children. Just proceed with caution. Wherever possible, help the other person take responsibility for themselves. You can always love and support, but do not allow another's crisis to drown you. You must survive to be helpful. Martyrdom is not something you do. It is something that happens because of what you value.

Relationships are a resource that provide things you cannot get elsewhere. They give you unique knowledge, perspectives, and a sense of belonging. Close relationships provide the most valuable thing in the world—perspective on yourself. The closest relationships provide love and meaning.

Different people see the world through different lenses. Even twins' minds and experiences are unique and original. This gives each person a unique knowledge of the world. This does not mean that all people's perspectives are correct or valuable. It is your job to find the valuable, useful, and meaningful perspectives. Hopefully, they exist in the employees you hire, bosses you choose, spouse you marry, friends you gain, and the way you raise your children. These relationships give access to perspectives you can share.

Close relationships provide love and meaning as you internalize and integrate their perspectives. In marriage, you become one with another person, integrating with them physically, mentally, emotionally, and spiritually. Likewise, relationships with your children cause you to grow up. Children expect excellent parents. This expectation can bring out the best in you, as you consider what it means to be a father and mother and the critical importance of both.

Relationships tell you about yourself. You can read brilliant thinkers, listen to skilled speakers, and enjoy entertainment by talented storytellers. These provide knowledge and perspective, and they can tell you about yourself in a meta-sense or human sense by drawing parallels across the human experience. What they cannot do is teach you about yourself individually because they do not know you individually. Your friends, family, and associates know you. The more open, honest, and transparent you are, the better perspective you get from others. They can help you see blind spots and point out your ignorance. They can cheer your genius, love you for who you are becoming, and forgive you when you mess up.

Out of relationships come new things. Physically, a man and woman can conceive a child. Ideas and mental work combine to make telescopes, steam engines, cotton gins, light bulbs, and personal computers. Almost all top-quality entertainment is founded on an emotional, relational combination. Within a band, drums build rhythm, guitar creates melody, and bass connects the rhythm to root notes. Charisma between actors creates powerful plays, movies, and television shows. Spiritual connection in the church is responsible for grand architecture, art, and music of the past; schools and hospitals; raising the status of women by condemning infidelity, divorce, incest, and polygamy; protected children by condemning infanticide and abortion; and brought human progress to science, medicine, arts, literature, politics, philosophy, ethics, and business. This is the power of relationships. Your relationships matter—they are your most important resource, so invest in them.

Investing in Relationships

How do you invest in relationships? It starts by choosing the right relationships. Of course, this is not always possible. Work limits your options, you do not pick your children, and you do not have absolute control over your neighbors. Because relationships are an important resource, choose the right relationships and avoid investing your heart without understanding the consequences.

To invest in relationships, you must be stable. The person with an unhealthy need of another person is unstable. This manifests in needy boyfriends and jealous girlfriends. At deeper levels, it is seen in those dependent on the state and children raised by overprotective parents. You have little to offer if you cannot stand on your own. If you are uncomfortable telling your boss no, rejecting sexual advances, or turning down offered help, then you will struggle to choose the right relationships. Get yourself in order first.

Choosing right relationships is not about choosing perfect

relationships. Do not let perfection be the enemy of good. If you have something to offer a relationship and the relationship has something to offer you, good! This is balanced. If you need something from the relationship and the relationship needs nothing from you, expect difficulty. In such a relationship, you give another power over you. If you have something to offer the relationship but it has nothing for you— more difficulty.

When you have a balanced relationship, you can invest in it. In a difficult relationship, one person invests with no return. Eventually, resentment will creep into the unbalanced relationship. You cannot take out of a relationship more than you put into it. Likewise, you will not value a relationship that does not value your investment. Judge how much give and take is likely before entering a relationship. Seneca's advice is prudent:

> If you are looking on anyone as a friend when you do not trust
> him as you trust yourself, you are making a grave mistake and
> have failed to grasp sufficiently the full force of true friendship.
> Certainly, you have discussed everything with a friend; but before
> you do so, discuss in your mind the man himself. After friendship
> is formed you must trust, but before that, you must judge. Those
> people who judge a man after they have made him their friend
> instead of the other way around certainly put the cart before the
> horse. Think for a long time whether you should admit a given
> person to your friendship.

Second, invest in relationships along the four paradigms of being. Invest physically with your presence, mentally with your words, emotionally with your actions, and spiritually with your attention, will, and prayer.

Physical relational investment is important, particularly at the beginning. You cannot minimize time with children. The value of time with your children is incalculable because childhood is limited. Of course, quality time is important, but quantity *is* quality with children.

Solidly built and established relationships can withstand long absences and lack of presence. You see this when two best friends meet up after a few years apart.

Part of physical relationship investing is the nature of the physical investment. Some people value a hug or firm handshake; for others, this is uncomfortable. Some value gifts, others prefer acts of kindness. Gary Chapman's *The 5 Love Languages* lays out the different ways you show and receive love. Ultimately love is about presence, whether in time shopping for the right gift or sitting on the couch and listening. Chapman's website (5lovelanguages.com) is a great resource for discovering how you communicate and receive love.

Mental investment is choosing loyalty to a relationship, which is logical. Physical separation happens. You may lose emotional or spiritual connection, but you still choose them. You judge and assent to the relationship regardless of the state of your relationship.

Be careful with mental investment, as such investment is easy. Not backing it up down the line has a cost. For example, when you break a promise to a child, you dramatically hurt the relationship. The child had a need and believed in your commitment to meeting that need. An unkept promise is not easily remedied. Never promise and mentally commit without delivering.

Loyalty is the same. People often assume loyalty. A friend drinks too much and feels hurt when you do not have their back. Is this disloyal? It is if you did not set the expectation up front. "Friend, I like you, but you drink too much. When you get wild, I cannot have your back." This is an honest, loyal statement. This is genuine friendship.

Finally, mental investment mandates listening deeply (see chapter 9). As discussed previously, true listening is more than just hearing.

Emotional investment requires courage to be honest. No relationship is perfect; honesty builds strong relationships. A lot can be said about picking your battles, but where you look for honesty, expect honesty. Trivial questions often mask a need for validation or a desire to test the fitness or confidence of a partner. It is often a trivial question that leads to a fight that masks underlying issues. Should you pick the battle or be honest? Be honest. Just don't use honesty to tear down. If not asked, keep your thoughts to yourself. Not every relationship seeks honest criticism at all times.

Emotional investment in a relationship can make a tremendous impact. You see this when people go through stressful situations together. The bond of soldiers in war is a prime example. A fear of death forces deeply emotional investment in one another. When you share your deep secrets, desires, lusts, angers, and fears with another, you risk rejection, betrayal, and pain, but you are being open and honest. In marriage, secret desires and lusts satiated by modern pornography or *50 Shades*-style erotica cripple emotional investment. Many are uncomfortable expressing themselves if their significant other takes the dishonest route. However, hiding emotionally challenging secrets is no way forward.

War and sexuality are extreme examples, but how often do you avoid emotional investments in professional relationships? You do not call out the boss on unwise decisions or correct lazy employees to avoid confrontation.

It takes wisdom to know when and how to approach these situations. The relationship might not need or want honest criticism; instead, it may need honest empathy. Further, if the relationship does not want honesty, but just acceptance, the honesty will do no good. The relationship may need you to withhold judgment and give love. Modern people seem more accepting than past generations, but this often hides incorrect judgments. The path forward is proper assent, not withholding judgment when you can tell right from wrong. Striking a healthy balance between judgment and acceptance also demands wisdom.

Spiritual investment is probably best understood by parents. How do you infuse spirit into a relationship, by putting the relationship ahead of yourself. You take the kids on adventures knowing they will be slow, complain, and lose their gear. You sacrifice, keep it together, and make it a good time no matter what! When you're tired, emotionally drained, and unable to concentrate, you still listen to your child. You invest at spirit level when you do these things. This is the spark of discipline being ignited in you. You do not shy away from hard conversations. You call out destructive behavior and cheer the genius; you are present, engaged in the process, and modeling the divine for the other person. There is nothing like parenting to cause you to rise to the occasion!

Allowing Investment

If you follow Seneca's advice quoted in the last section, you will trust your friends as you trust yourself. If you invest in yourself, you should let others invest in you too.

Allowing this can be a struggle. You may not want to feel indebted to another person or feel someone has an advantage over you. You may dislike criticism and seldom want help.

Disliking criticism and avoiding help are selfish traits, evidence of super-ego, in Freudian terms. There is nothing wrong with debt handled in a reasonable and controlled way. There is nothing wrong with trusting another person with your life, if done in a careful and controlled way.

The best relationships are those in which you both have much to gain, not where one leans solely on the other. Why might you struggle trusting others with secrets? Why might you recoil at criticism instead of being thankful for an opportunity to learn and grow? Why might you shy away from sharing ideas and thoughts? How can you be a good listener and yet a bad talker? Shakespeare had Macbeth say, "Life . . . is a tale told by an idiot, full of sound and fury, signifying nothing." How true and sad for so many! Quiet the storm inside and listen to those around you.

Such humility shows a healthy self-esteem and allows others to invest in you. Self-esteem says you are worthy of investment, and humility says you have much yet to learn. Low self-esteem and arrogance are negative emotional reactions to others. Take the time to listen to others, as Jordan Peterson points out in *12 Rules for Life*, "Assume that the person you are listening to might know something you don't." Low self-esteem's natural reaction is defense.

It is never pleasant to come under attack. Part of your subconscious psyche wants to be affirmed. It does not want to be corrected. You may halt the individuation process and repress your personal and collective unconscious dreams, imaginations, and associations for fear of criticism and to protect your ego. It is common for large portions of these processes to be repressed. Ever wonder why people get angry in bad traffic, feel shame when their spouse catches them glancing at an attractive person, or bristle when the boss criticizes their work?

Let go of the ego and acknowledge the parts of you that are selfish, angry, lustful, greedy, and lazy. Let those who want to invest in you make you better and bear good fruit. When someone cheers, accept it in humility and keep up that cheer-worthy action. When someone listens, be honest. When someone invests in you, be grateful, but drop your ego at the door first.

Chapter 16

COMMUNITY RESOURCES

Government of the people, by the people, for the people, shall not perish from the earth.

—Abraham Lincoln

No matter what we achieve, if we don't spend the vast majority of our time with people we love and respect, we cannot possibly have a great life.

—Jim Collins

People

A community's resources include money, people, land, and natural resources. Business resources include technology, methods, trademarks, skills, and location. You cannot know all a community's resources. Not even a professional like a lawyer, doctor, or accountant, in which the professional holds substantial knowledge, knows all the details. Their associates or other staff members hold some resources.

For communities of hundreds or thousands of people, silos of information about resources and the utilization of those resources exist that are unique and unknown to the top of the knowledge hierarchy. Different resources spread across a community's members. In the context of a broader community perspective of towns, cities, states, nations, and the world, the problem of resource identification and utilization is complex beyond comprehension. There is no leader, president, chief, or CEO with a full understanding of a community's resources.

For a community to solve the problem of resource allocation and utilization, it cannot rely on top-down management. Autocratic rule always fails. The problem stems from the individual's ability to access and use needed resources for a needed or meaningful task. When President John F. Kennedy outlined the future of the space program, he did not know the needs; instead, he focused on creating an organization (NASA) that would involve the right people.

People are the most important resource. The more you liberate people, the better they can access and use resources in their area of expertise, at their location, and for others' benefit. Truly free people actively share, promote, and strive to bring freedom to others. The freer people are with their lives, hearts, minds, and spirits, the more they will seek, find, and use resources to accomplish meaningful objectives.

People know things, extract resources from the earth, craft items from nature, and imagine inventions out of thin air if given the freedom. The best a leader can do is to articulate vision or direction. A visionary leader can evangelize the goal of a community, but they must let the right people tell what is needed to get the job done, generate money, sell services, build buildings, and legislate laws. People are the crucial resource. However, you do not need just any people. You need the right people for the right job!

Who are the right people?

The Right People

"Get the right people on the bus!" This comes from Jim Collins's *Good to Great*. The principle is that people matter, and the right people matter even more. Good leadership that wants to become great focuses on people more than anything else. The direction of the bus matters, but not as much as having the right people onboard. A leader states what the purpose of the bus is—to start a community, generate revenue, stand against oppression, sell widgets, or improve lives. However, once the leader spells out how to get these things done, they stop needing people, and ego rears its head. The right people figure out how to move the bus toward a purpose.

So, who are the right people? Space is limited on a bus going to a meaningful destination. So, be selective. It is better to have an empty seat than a seat filled by the wrong person. For a business, an empty seat may mean a product does not get sold, and that could be bad; but a seat filled with the wrong person could mean the wrong product gets sold. Instead of fewer customers, angry customers tell others who become angry too! The wrong person is the wrong person. Seldom will you find a middle-ground person.

A mediocre person is the worst wrong person because they are a wrong person in hiding. A wrong person does the wrong things—it is obvious. They must go! Typically, the wrong person quits, although rarely soon enough. A mediocre person is the wrong person who is smart, tricky, or lucky enough not to stand out as the wrong person. They coast without being invested, but hide that fact. Mediocre people are cancerous, because they lure others into mediocrity.

A right person gets the job done. But getting the job done is the most basic step; mediocre people often get the job done too. What is different is how a right person gets the job done—early and under budget. They do the job plus another—and do each job a better way. The right person does the job with the right attitude, without being asked or told. This person does jobs that are not theirs and then asks for more jobs. They take less pay or do the same job in a way that adds value. The right person smiles at customers, holds doors open, and lives, acts, and thinks in meaningful ways about the work that needs to get done. The right person often creates their own job, working themselves out of their current job and into one where personal value is maximized. The right person does not need an outstanding leader or manager or the perfect community, company, or organization. The right person flourishes wherever they are.

Finding the right person is about finding a person with character! When assessing for character, give the person a problem and observe how they solve it. People with character deal with obstacles in healthy ways. Ask about problems they have faced in their lives; question when they experienced discomfort or met barriers. A person with character is realistic about their weaknesses. Follow questions about strengths with questions about weaknesses. Does the person have strong ethics? Are they conscientious? Finally, a person with character seeks meaning in life!

A mediocre person gets the job done, but should be off the bus. Kicking someone off is hard in the midst of the nitty-gritty of everyday life. You can mistakenly think certain employees are mediocre—dishwasher, custodian, fast-food worker, etc. These jobs are not rocket science and are almost fail-proof. All the mediocre person must do is show up and follow a step-by-step to-do list. This is often all mediocre leadership wants: someone to show up and do the job. When someone fulfills this base need, mediocre leadership settles. Yes, you are mediocre when you settle! With mediocre expectations, it is easy to make excuses. Granted, your excuses could be legitimate, and you must pick your battles.

You cannot include or exclude all of the margin. A town may not run out of mediocre people, and a business may not eliminate every mediocre employee. However, work toward that goal while leaving grace at the margins. Before you worry about the broader communities, ask if you are developing yourself and close relationships. Research how you can deal with entrenched governmental laws and regulations that codify mediocrity in government, civil service, and education. The person protesting the government who cannot excel in their own work life is evil.

Humans tend toward mediocrity and laziness. It is easy to denigrate government, bureaucratic big business, and education without pulling your own life together and those in your immediate circle of influence. Expecting more from your communities does not mean talking down to everyone. It means living as a better example.

Right people are not those who make no mistakes. They may get the job done, but they may also fail. The reason they fail is that they walk the line between chaos and order. They push themselves to grow, adapt, and better things. As a result, when they accomplish a job, they also add value.

The more freedom you can give a person, the more the person learns and grows. However, the right person often makes mistakes until they figure things out. You can quickly ascertain whether the person failed for right or wrong reasons. If the person takes responsibility for the failure, the failure was for the right reason: learning. If they blame customers, vendors, associates, organizations, the weather, war, God, or anything or anyone else at all, this person is mediocre or worse. The right person adds value and works on positioning. They are considering the fourth principle of the environment.

Finally, the right person lives by the five principles in this book. The right person does something meaningful, for which they are developing needed skills while positioning to add value and being conscientious about time and resources.

This also applies to larger communities, though it is harder to focus on the right people in larger organizations. Our backward age incentivizes stupidity, laziness, and easy. Search for "fast weight loss" on the internet and you instantly get 659 million results focused on diet pills, detox teas, diet cleansing, and other nonsense. Mentalities that lower expectations are unhealthy. Address this by focusing on expectations of yourself and your circle of influence.

Promote right people by expecting right people. Communicate expectations in clear, measurable, attainable, and realistic ways. Society does not expect exceptional people, but this is not society's fault. It is your fault. It is my fault.

Everyone thinks of changing the world, but nobody thinks of changing himself. (Leo Tolstoy)

Abundance Vs. Scarcity

Stop living with a scarcity mindset. The world is producing more and more, hunger is down, incomes are up, and new breakthroughs are seen in energy, medicine, and technology daily!

You live in a time of superabundance. Our children can make the world better by innovating and reducing resource scarcity. Broad evidence points to humanity's ability to improve the world when coupled with reason and faith. To what extent? Only your children and their children will know; but if you teach them that things are scarce, to be careful, not to expect much or to compete, and to live in fear, they will not go far.

Ongoing research shows the growth of abundance on this planet. Take, for example, the decline in cost of a Thanksgiving dinner. It is dropping faster than population growth in America. The price of the most elaborate, expensive, and detailed meal prepared by Americans is on a continuous decline. Thanks to this trend, more Americans can more easily take part in a superabundant celebration of Thanksgiving. Recent calculations confirm what University of Maryland economist Julian Simon observed in *The Ultimate Resource*: when people use their minds and apply focus, discipline, and innovation, they find new efficiencies and can decrease shortages, increase supply, and invent substitutes. This is known as the "Simon Abundance Index" (Pooley and Tupy 2021).

When you question your life purpose, when you feel you can do nothing meaningful, when you do not value others, and when you misunderstand your place in the world, you horde resources—bury them in the ground or hide them under the bed. If humans lived with purpose, worked to develop skill, built relationships, valued others, and positioned themselves to add value in the environment, humanity would view resources as abundant, growable, and useful for reducing suffering. You live in a world of abundance; you have the time, money, and resources to make a difference if you invest and spend those moments and other resources in disciplined ways.

PART VI
PURPOSE
REVISITED

A meaningful and fruitful life.

Chapter 17

UNIFICATION AND INTERNALIZATION

Live purposefully. Work to develop skill. Build relationships and value people. Position yourself to add value. Be disciplined about the utilization of resources.

—Christopher Clay

Combining the Principles

Each principle in *Five Principles* can stand alone. You can have meaning without skill. Your purpose could be in finance or you could be a skilled musician. There can be purpose in doing something for the sake of doing it, especially rest and recuperation. You can have relationships because you enjoy people, even though they have no correlation with your purpose in life.

However, the strength of the five principles comes where they overlap. Typically, purpose dictates needed skills, relationships, environment, and resources. However, any single principle can dictate meaning and growth in the other principles. Where there is more overlap, you will have greater impact. You can change principles and have a large or narrow purpose. One purpose can affect millions, while another affects a few or just one.

The more you unify your life principles, the better you will walk your path. Where purpose, skill, people, environment, and resources become one, the path straightens.

For the samurai who aims to bring peace, learning the way of the sword is a skill. However, combat is not just swordsmanship; combat is understanding people, terrain, and resources. The supreme samurai practices swordsmanship alongside diplomacy, politics, healthy relationships, and development of mind, body, heart, and spirit. The purpose is infused in the sword, people, environment, and disciplined use of each day. The samurai who defends only himself practices an empty skill.

Apply this to the modern mind or your daily job. You do the job because it is cool or pays the bills. However, when you realize paying the bills is "the way of the sword," you get good at it. Yet when do you realize that your job is "the way" and not just a job—that your family, friends, and communities you serve are all "the way"? When do you use your skills, relationships, environment, and resources to maximize the meaningfulness of what you do at work, home, and in relationships?

Those are hard questions. Start answering them. Seek guides. Find something meaningful to aim toward and take one step at a time. You will stumble, fall, learn, and grow toward what is meaningful. Look beyond yourself. Do something emotionally challenging, mentally challenging, and physically challenging.

A lawyer, accountant, doctor, nurse, clerk, janitor, or sanitation worker who realizes their job has purpose, that they can be skilled at it and serve others through it, is positioned to add value at work. They uses all the resources at their disposal on the path. Your job may be caring for a spouse, parent, neighbor, church elder, or community member. Or it may be bringing peace, helping the poor, visiting the elderly, or writing a poem. If done in a meaningful, skilled, people-focused, well-positioned, resourceful way, it is on the path.

You can unify the five principles as you refine your ability to live a meaningful life. You can get better at defining your purpose, honing your skills, relating to people, positioning yourself, and using resources to move toward what is meaningful. Often this is the only way to move forward.

How can you position yourself in the environment if you stay locked in your own room, mind, or heart? You can't. Step into the world and navigate the risks, being thankful for pain that teaches. Follow others who went before you, allowing them to lighten the load.

In living a meaningful life, you will find two things. First, your meaningful life is individual. Second, others have lived meaningful lives similar to yours. So, take heart. You are not alone in seeking a meaningful, fruitful life.

You may try to dictate purpose, skill, people, environment, and resources, but do not fear when they dictate themselves. There is a fine balance between chaos and order. Alcoholics Anonymous gives us the serenity prayer: "God grant me the serenity to accept the things I cannot change, courage to change the things I can, and wisdom to know the difference."

Making the Principles Your Own

How do you live purposefully, develop skills, build relationships, value people, position yourself to add value, and maintain discipline about resource utilization? Start with a blank piece of paper. Write down the hardest items first and work backward from there.

- What can you do that is more important or bigger than yourself?
- What can you do to improve your body, heart, mind, and spirit?
- How can you put your body, heart, mind, and spirit out there every day?
- What are your jobs—in your work, family, friends, neighbors, community, and church?
  - How can you serve these people?
  - What skills do these people need? What skills can you use to help deliver what these people need?
  - How can you position yourself in the environment—geographically, work, family, etc.?

- What are your resources? Break them down on paper: work hours; sleep hours; money spent on X, Y, and Z; money saved; people; knowledge; etc.

These questions are just examples. You internalize the five principles and build a framework by which to live when you make them tangible. As you further understand yourself, people, and the world, you develop an understanding of your mission in life. You may have multiple purposes. Maybe you have a single purpose.

As you align these five principles over the coming days, weeks, months, and years, the results will amaze you. Your skills will improve and become needed, your position will improve, time will open for use, people will value you, your purpose will become clearer, and your life will change. Life becomes harder but more meaningful. Like the slave who becomes leader of a house, prison, and ultimately a nation, responsibility increases, accompanied by stress. The demands on the body, heart, mind, and spirit will grow and grow.

Unfortunately, the more meaningful your path, the more resentment and hate you encounter. Accumulating enemies is expected on this path. Jesus Christ warned his disciples, "I send you out as sheep in the midst of wolves. Therefore be wise as serpents and harmless as doves" (Matthew 1:16 NKJV). Be careful about advertising your path. The serpent does not get prey that sees it coming.

Ultimate Purpose

As you combine purpose, skill, people, environment, and resources, seeing the ways they overlap and incorporating them into your life, define them. Define your ultimate purpose, your mission, or your vision statement. This overarching goal encompasses all the other, more specific goals and objectives in life. For example, you may have goals of being a healthy person, good spouse, good employee, and good community member. (Note: actual goals should be more precise. Refer to SMART goals for details in chapter 14.) Great! However, these goals do not answer your overall, ultimate purpose.

This comes from where you find yourself today. You are who you are, partly because of the time and place of your existence. However, ultimate purpose does not completely come from where you find yourself. You are not all nature; you are, in part, nurture. You are growing and being created. You can adapt, change, and move. You have free will. You must consider your aspirations, desires, and wishes—secret, unconscious, and otherwise. You were not a perfect baby with perfect parents, and no generation before you was perfect.

You are at inner war, battling with or against your ultimate purpose. In part, you never live up to your own standards; you will fail, suffer unhappiness, and deal with feelings of meaninglessness. This inner war is because you sense what Cicero called *summum bonum* (highest good), which Plato termed "the form of the good"—the ultimate purpose that gives true meaning.

Your ultimate purpose considers all the purposeful things in life: your skills, relationships, environmental position, and available resources. It is aspirational, pushing you to become more than you are today. Rewrite it as you gain clarity, but do this rarely. It should push you toward action, toward a legacy pointing to something more meaningful than yourself. Define and refine your purpose in life until it points beyond you to ultimate meaning.

Ultimate purpose is not of this world. It is an act of God's grace that we can see purpose at all. Therefore, ultimate purpose is bound up in God's grace. As a child of God, my ultimate purpose begins where I fail. This does not mean life is purposeless. There is purpose in learning obedience to God, giving him my heart, and pointing to his glory. The Hebrew scriptures frequently reference stones being stood up to remind people of God's work. The lives of God's children are standing stones pointing to him.

Chapter 18

GETTING STARTED

The secret of getting ahead is getting started.

—Mark Twain

The greatest danger for most of us is not that our aim is too high and we miss it, but that it is too low and we reach it.

—Michelangelo

Hit the Ground Running

Once bad life patterns and habits become integrated and natural, breaking them is a difficult task. Hypnotists, faith healers, and motivational speakers use adrenaline, influence, and emotional engagement to interrupt people's patterns and make them believe change occurred. With live audiences, these changes rarely last. To change your life, engage yourself physically, mentally, emotionally, and spiritually in the desired change.

Here are six quick ways to disrupt your patterns and jump-start positive change. The following points are designed to connect meaningfully with your body, heart, mind, and spirit.

1. Write a purpose statement or revise your mission statement. Consider creating a legacy more meaningful than yourself. Meditate and pray about your purpose in life.

2. Develop a skill. Find a useful skill and build it. Plan out the skill development—books to read, seminars to attend, and teachers. Make sure you begin!

3. Control emotions. Recognize what makes you emotional. Consider eliminating unhealthy activities that make you feel too good. Tell the truth even when it hurts, and share something that puts you at risk for emotional pain.

4. Take ownership of the most important relationships in your life. Whether with a spouse, child, parent, boss, coworker, or employee, act as if you are responsible for the outcome, emotions, and thoughts within the relationship. (Remember, you are ultimately responsible only for yourself.) Do this without the other person knowing. When you fail at getting the best outcome for the other person, do not react emotionally.

5. Try changing position. Look where you are today along a line of being within your work, family, or community environment. Compare where you are to where you could be at a specific time in the future that would be meaningful. What could you do to move within that environment toward a place of more value and meaning? Write it down and begin!

6. Account for a resource. Many people want to begin with money, because society defines this as success. However, time is a better resource. Track your time and be disciplined about priority and focus. Always have a plan for the month, week, day, and hour. Think about how time can be better used toward your purpose, development of skill, service of people, and meaningful movement within your environment.

A meaningful and fruitful life.

BIBLIOGRAPHY

Basu S, Berkowitz SA, Phillips RL, Bitton A, Landon BE, Phillips RS. Published online February 18, 2019. "Association of Primary Care Physician Supply With Population Mortality in the United States, 2005-2015." JAMA Intern Med. doi:10.1001/jamainternmed.201.

Basu, Tanya. 2021. "Human Behavioral Complexity Peaks at Age 25." 07 06. https://www.inverse.com/article/30295-human-behavioral-complexity-fast-random-decision.

Collins, Jim. 2001. *Good to Great*. New York, NY: HarperCollins Inc.

Contributors, Wikipedia. 2022. "We choose to go to the Moon" - Wikipedia. July 3. Accessed July 25, 2022. https://en.wikipedia.org/w/index.php?title=We_choose_to_go_to_the_Moon&oldid=1096330096.

Covey, Stephen R. 1989. *The 7 Habits of Highly Effective People*. pp 188-202. New York: Free Press.

Cummins, Eleanor. 2021. "3 Life-Changing Things That Happen to the Human Brain at 25." 07 06. https://www.inverse.com/article/33753-brain-changes-health-25-quarter-life-crisis-neurology.

Delbert, Caroline. 2020. "Sad! This Is When the Universe Will Truly End." 9 24. https://www.popularmechanics.com/space/deep-space/a33612633/when-will-the-universe-end/.

Epictetus. n.d. *The Manual: A Philosopher's Guide to Life (Stoic Philosophy Book 1)*. Kindle Edition. Edited by Sam Torode. Ancient Renewal.

Flynn, James. 2020. "How We Know Humans Are Getting Smarter" (Excerpt). 12 02. https://www.scientificamerican.com/article/how-we-know-humans-getting-smarter-flynn-excerpt/.

Hajcak, Greg. 2021. "The Clinical Neuroscience of Mistakes." 07 06. https://www.apa.org/science/about/psa/2016/02/clinical-neuroscience.

Huberman, Ander. 2021. Podcasts. 07 06. https://hubermanlab.com/category/podcast-episodes/.

Jarrett, Christian. 2016. "The Psychology of Eye Contact, Digested." 11 28. https://digest.bps.org.uk/2016/11/28/the-psychology-of-eye-contact-digested/.

GO DEEPER

Want exclusive content and access to a private online community
of like-minded individuals?
Visit **tinyurl.com/5principlesassent** today!

Interested in summaries of these topics or a deeper discussion?
Check out the **TheAssentPodcast.com**.

Hungry for additional articles or resources to grow as an individual,
have better relationships, and be a leader in your community?
It's all available at **TheFivePrinciples.com**.